Preparing Instructional Objectives

Revised Second Edition

Robert F. Mager

Lake Publishing Company
Belmont, California

BOOKS BY ROBERT F. MAGER

Preparing Instructional Objectives, *Revised Second Edition*

Measuring Instructional Results, *Second Edition*

Analyzing Performance Problems, *Second Edition*
(with Peter Pipe)

Goal Analysis, *Second Edition*

Developing Attitude Toward Learning, *Second Edition*

Making Instruction Work

Developing Vocational Instruction
(with Kenneth Beach)

Troubleshooting the Troubleshooting Course

Library of Congress Catalog Card Number: 83-60503
Printed in the United States of America

2.9

Contents

Preface *v*

1 **Objectives** *1*
    (*What the book is about*)

2 **Why Care About Objectives?** *5*
    (*Importance of being explicit*)

3 **The Qualities of Useful Objectives** *19*
    (*Do they communicate?*)

4 **Performance** *23*
    (*What will the learner be doing?*)

5 **Conditions** *49*
    (*What conditions will you impose?*)

6 **Criterion** *71*
    (*How will you recognize success?*)

7 **Pitfalls and Barnacles** *89*
    (*Common problems*)

8 **Sharpen Your Skill** *105*
    (*Guided practice*)

9 **Self-Test** *123*
    (*How well did you do?*)

The Stoner and the Stonees *135*

Note

Much of this book has been put together differently from most books you have read. On many pages you will be asked a question. When this happens, select the best answer, and then turn to the page referred to beside that answer. This way, you read only the material that applies to your needs, and you can proceed without being distracted by unnecessary explanations.

Preface

       Once upon a time a Sea Horse gathered up his seven pieces of eight and cantered out to find his fortune. Before he had traveled very far he met an Eel, who said,

"Psst. Hey, bud. Where 'ya goin'?"

"I'm going out to find my fortune," replied the Sea Horse, proudly.

"You're in luck," said the Eel. "For four pieces of eight you can have this speedy flipper, and then you'll be able to get there a lot faster."

"Gee, that's swell," said the Sea Horse, and paid the money and put on the flipper and slithered off at twice the speed. Soon he came upon a Sponge, who said,

"Psst. Hey, bud. Where 'ya goin'?"

"I'm going out to find my fortune," replied the Sea Horse.

"You're in luck," said the Sponge. "For a small fee I will let you have this jet-propelled scooter so that you will be able to travel a lot faster."

So the Sea Horse bought the scooter with his remaining money and went zooming thru the sea five times as fast. Soon he came upon a Shark, who said,

"Psst. Hey, bud. Where 'ya goin'?"

"I'm going to find my fortune," replied the Sea Horse.

"You're in luck. If you'll take this short cut," said the Shark, pointing to his open mouth, "you'll save yourself a lot of time."

"Gee, thanks," said the Sea Horse, and zoomed off into the interior of the Shark, and was never heard from again.

The moral of this fable is that if you're not sure where you're going, you're liable to end up someplace else.

Before you prepare instruction, before you select instructional procedures or subject matter or material, it is important to be able to state clearly just what you intend the results of that instruction to be. A clear statement of instructional objectives will provide a sound basis for choosing methods and materials and for selecting the means for assessing whether the instruction has been successful. This book is about the characteristics of well-stated objectives. It will describe and illustrate how to prepare objectives that communicate your instructional intents to yourself and to others. You will be offered some guided practice along the way, as well as a chance to test your skill at the end of the book.

This book is NOT about *who* should select objectives, nor is it about *how* one goes about deciding which objectives are worth teaching. These are important questions, but they are beyond the scope of this book.

It is assumed that you are interested in preparing effective instruction, that you are interested in communicating certain skills and knowledge to your students, and in communicating them in such a way that your students will be able to demonstrate their achievement of the objectives that you or someone else has selected for them to achieve. (If you are *not* interested in demonstrating achievement of your objectives, you have just finished this book.)

ROBERT F. MAGER

Carefree, Arizona
January, 1984

1 ‖ Objectives

Instruction is effective to the degree that it succeeds in:

- changing students
- in desired directions
- and not in undesired directions.

If instruction doesn't change anyone, it has no effect, no power. If it changes a student in undesired, rather than in desired, directions (that is, if it has unwanted side effects, such as squashing motivation), it isn't called effective; instead, it is called poor, undesirable, or even harmful instruction. Instruction is successful, or effective, to the degree that it accomplishes what it sets out to accomplish.

Once you decide to teach someone something, several kinds of activity are indicated if your instruction is to be successful. For one thing, you must assure yourself that there is a need for the instruction, making certain that (1) your students don't already know what you intend to teach and (2) instruction is the best means for bringing about a desired change. For another, you must clearly specify the outcomes or objectives you intend your instruction to accomplish. You must select and arrange learning experiences for your students in accordance with principles of learning and must evaluate student performance according to the objectives originally selected. In other words, first you decide where you want to go, then you create and administer the means of getting there, and then you arrange to find out whether you arrived.

The steps for accomplishing this arrange themselves into these three phases—analysis, design, and implementation—and a number of procedures and techniques are available through which to complete them. The analysis phase, for example, should answer questions such as these:

Is there a problem worth solving?

Is instruction a relevant part of the solution?

If so, what should the instruction accomplish?

After all, instruction is only one of several possible solutions to problems of human performance and not even the one most often called for. Unless a suitable analysis is performed *before* instruction is developed, it is quite possible to construct a magnificent course that doesn't help anybody at all. It is possible to construct a course that nobody needs, either because instruction is unrelated to solving the problem that gave rise to it or because it "teaches" things the students already know. Techniques such as performance analysis[1] and goal analysis[2] can help avoid such wasteful practices.

After the analysis is completed (it may take only a few minutes, or a few months), if the analysis reveals that instruction is needed, objectives are drafted that describe the important outcomes intended to be accomplished by that instruction. In other words, objectives are drafted that answer the question "What is worth teaching?" Instruments (tests) are then drafted by which the success of the instruction can be assessed.

Only after the preceding steps have been completed is the actual instruction drafted, tested, revised, and then put into use. And, please note, only after the analysis phase is complete or near completion are objectives drafted. This is an important point because when you read or hear that "the first thing you do is write objectives" or "objectives are written before instruction is designed," you should translate that into "*after* the analysis is completed, *then* objectives are prepared *before* the instruction is designed."

---

1. See *Analyzing Performance Problems, Second Edition*, R. F. Mager and Peter Pipe (David S. Lake Publishers, 1984).
2. See *Goal Analysis, Second Edition*, R. F. Mager (David S. Lake Publishers, 1984).

An *objective* is a description of a performance you want learners to be able to exhibit before you consider them competent. An objective describes an intended *result* of instruction, rather than the *process* of instruction itself.

This book is concerned with the *characteristics* of a usefully stated objective, rather than with its derivation or selection. The purpose of the book is limited to helping you specify and communicate those instructional intents you or someone else has decided are worth achieving. If this book achieves its objective, you will be able to recognize the characteristics of well-stated objectives when they are present. Once you can recognize desirable characteristics, you will be able to prepare your own objectives by modifying your drafts until they are well stated.

Specifically:

Given any objective in a subject area with which you are familiar, in all instances be able to identify (label) *correctly the* PERFORMANCE, *the* CONDITIONS, *and the* CRITERION *of acceptable performance when any or all those characteristics are present.*

To help you reach this objective, I will describe some of the advantages to be gained from the careful specification of objectives, describe and illustrate the characteristics of a usefully stated objective, and give you some practice in recognizing such objectives. At the end, you will have an opportunity to determine just how well our efforts have succeeded.

2 | Why Care About Objectives?

An *objective* is a description of a performance you want learners to be able to exhibit before you consider them competent. An objective describes an intended *result* of instruction, rather than the *process* of instruction itself.

Explicit objectives are important for a number of reasons. Here are three of the main ones: First, when clearly defined objectives are lacking, there is no sound basis for the selection or designing of instructional materials, content, or methods. If you don't know where you're going, it is difficult to select a suitable means for getting there. After all, machinists and surgeons don't select tools until they know what operation they are going to perform. Neither do composers orchestrate scores until they know the effects they are trying to achieve. Similarly, builders don't select materials or specify schedules for construction until they have their blueprints (objectives) before them. Too often, however, one hears instructors arguing the relative merits of textbooks *versus* filmstrips or of classrooms *versus* laboratories without ever specifying just what they expect the method or procedure to accomplish. Instructors simply function in a fog of their own making unless they know what they want their students to accomplish as a result of their instruction.

A second important reason for stating objectives sharply has to do with finding out whether the objective has, in fact, been accomplished. Tests or examinations are the mileposts along the road of learning and are supposed to tell instructors and students alike whether they have been successful in achieving the course objectives. But unless objectives are clearly and firmly fixed in the minds of both parties, tests are at best misleading; at worst, they are irrelevant, unfair, or uninformative. (How many courses have you taken in which tests had little or nothing to do with the substance of the instruction?) Test items designed to measure whether important instructional outcomes have been accomplished can be selected or created intelligently only when those instructional outcomes have been made explicit.

A third advantage of clearly defined objectives is that they provide students with the means to organize their own efforts toward accomplishment of those objectives. Experience has shown that with clear objectives in view, students at all levels are better able to decide what activities on their part will help them get to where it is important for them to go. When instructional intent is clarified by objectives, it is no longer necessary to "psych out" the instructor. As you know too well, many students spend considerable time and effort in learning the peculiarities of their instructors when those instructors fail or refuse to let students in on the secret of what they are expected to learn. Unfortunately, this knowledge is often useful to students with "school savvy." They may breeze through the instruction with no more than a bagful of tricks designed to rub the instructor the right way, wasting time that could have been used to learn something more useful.

Objectives, then, are useful in providing a sound basis (1) for the selection or designing of instructional content and procedures, (2) for evaluating or assessing the success of the instruction, and (3) for organizing the students' own efforts and activities for the accomplishment of the important instructional intents. In short, if you know where you are going, you have a better chance of getting there.

There are additional advantages, not the least important of which is that the drafting of objectives causes one to think seriously and deeply about what is worth teaching, about what is worth spending time and effort to accomplish. And if objectives are drafted that describe a course or curriculum already in existence, the objectives can serve as a spotlight to illuminate the worth of that existing instruction, and they can provide a basis for improving it.

A BASIC DISTINCTION

Before looking in detail at the characteristics of a usefully stated objective, it would be well to make sure we are thinking about the same thing. Always remember, an objective is a statement describing an instructional outcome rather than an instructional process or procedure. It describes intended results rather than the means of achieving those results.

Now look at the following statement, and then answer the question that comes after it. Turn to the page referred to beside the response you select:

A general survey of the organizing and administration of elementary- and secondary-school libraries, with emphasis on methods of developing the library as an integral part of the school. Includes functions, organization, services, equipment, and materials.

What does the above statement represent? Does the statement look more like an *objective* of a course, or does it look more like a *description* of a course?

An objective of a course.   **Turn to page 11.**

A description of a course.   **Turn to page 13.**

Here is an example of how, when objectives aren't stated carefully, activities in the classroom can hinder the student's efforts to achieve an objective.

At a large training establishment operated by the government, a course was once offered in which students were to learn how to operate and repair a big, complex electronic system. The goal of the course was simply stated: To be able to operate and maintain the XYZ Electronic System.

Since it was impossible (because of the exorbitant cost) to provide each student with a separate system to practice on, it was decided to increase the amount of troubleshooting students did during the course by giving them some "practice" in the classroom as well as in the laboratory.

During the classroom troubleshooting exercises, the instructor would pose various problems for the students to solve. He would point out a component on one of the many schematic diagrams of the equipment and ask, "What would happen if this tube were bad?" Students would then trace through the circuitry (on paper) in an effort to divine the symptoms that would appear as a result of the instructor's hypothetical trouble. The students were given a trouble and asked to induce symptoms.

This procedure, however, was exactly opposite to that which was expected of the learners on the final examination or on the job. There they were typically shown a symptom and asked to locate the trouble. The instructors were expecting learners to run forward by teaching them how to run backward.

Thus, for want of a specific statement of objectives, students were not only learning the wrong thing, but the habits they were developing in the classroom were in conflict with those they were expected to use on the job.

Ooooops! You didn't follow instructions. Nowhere in this book are you directed to this page. When you are asked a question, you are to select what you think is the correct or appropriate alternative and turn to the page indicated beside that alternative.

You see, I am trying to tailor my comments to your needs by asking you to answer some questions as we go. This way, it will not be necessary to bore you with additional explanations when a single one will do.

But, as long as you are here, you might as well run your eyeballs across the page opposite; then go back a page and read the instructions again.

Occasionally you will find material presented in italics on a left-hand page. This is auxiliary material that you may find interesting, informative, or useful. Read it as you go, or, if you find that distracting, save it for a rainy day.

You said the statement was an objective of a course. Apparently I didn't make myself clear earlier, so let me try again.

A course *description* tells you something about the content and procedures of a course. A course *objective* describes a desired outcome of a course. Perhaps the sketch below will help make the distinction clear:

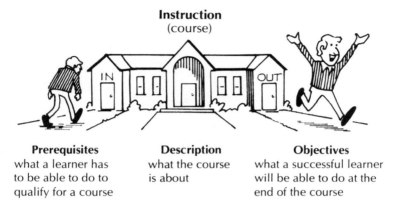

Instruction
(course)

Prerequisites	**Description**	**Objectives**
what a learner has to be able to do to qualify for a course	what the course is about	what a successful learner will be able to do at the end of the course

Whereas an objective tells what the learner will be able to perform as a result of some learning experiences, the course description tells only what the course is about.

The distinction is quite important because a course description does not explain what will be accepted as adequate achievement. Though a course description might tell students which field they will be playing on, it doesn't tell them where the boundary lines are, where the goalposts are located, or how they will know when they have scored.

It is useful to be able to recognize the difference between an objective and a description, so try another example.

Which of the following statements looks most like an *objective*?

In at least two computer languages, be able to write and test a program to calculate arithmetic means. *Turn to page 15.*

Discusses and illustrates principles and techniques of computer programming. *Turn to page 17.*

Suppose I offered to sell you an automobile for $500, and suppose I claimed that this auto was in excellent condition but refused to let you take a look at it. Would you buy it?

Suppose I offered to teach your children to be <u>Logical Thinkers</u> for $1,000. Now, if I could do it, you would be getting a real bargain. But would you agree to such a bargain unless I told you beforehand more explicitly what I intended to accomplish and how I would measure my success? I hope not.

In a sense, instructors make contracts with their students. The students agree to pay a certain sum of money and effort in return for certain skills and knowledge. But most of the time they are expected to pay for something that is never carefully defined or described. They are asked to buy (with effort) a product that they are not allowed to see and that is only vaguely described. Instructors who don't clearly specify their instructional objectives, who don't describe to the best of their ability what they intend the learner to be able to do after their instruction, are certainly taking unfair advantage of their students.

You said the statement was a description of a course. And right you are! I'm sure you recognized the statement as a course description lifted from a college catalog.

One final word about course descriptions before moving on. Though a description sometimes tells us a good deal about what a course includes, it does not tell us what the course is supposed to accomplish. More important, it does not tell us how to recognize when the intended outcomes have been achieved.

So, though a course description may be perfectly legitimate for a catalog, here we are interested *only* in the intended *results* of that course.

Zip ahead to page 19.

You said "in at least two computer languages, be able to write and test a program to calculate arithmetic means" was a statement of an objective.

Correct! The statement describes an intended outcome—something the student is expected to be able to do—rather than the procedure by which the student will develop that skill.

Since you can tell the difference between a course description and a course outcome, it's time to move on.

Turn to page 19.

A few years ago, the chief instructor of a 32-week military course noticed the peculiar fact that students were doing rather poorly on every third examination. Scores were low on the first exam and then considerably better on the next two, low on the fourth and high on the next two, and so on. Since scores were consistently low and then high even for the brighter students, the instructor correctly concluded that this peculiarity was not because of student intelligence or the lack of it. He then decided that he was so close to the course he probably wasn't seeing the woods for the trees, so he called in consultants.

During their analysis of the situation, the consultants noticed that the course was divided into five subcourses. Each subcourse was taught by a different team of instructors, and during each subcourse the students were given three examinations. They discovered that students did poorly on the first test because they hadn't been told what to expect; they had to use the first test as a means of finding out what the instructors expected. Once they had learned what the objectives were, they did much better on the next two exams of that subcourse. But then another team of instructors took over. Believing the second team's examinations would be similar to those of the first team, the students prepared themselves accordingly, only to discover that the rules had been changed without their knowledge. They then did poorly on the fourth test (the first test given by the new instructor team). And so it went throughout the course. Objectives were vague, and the students were never told what to expect.

Once these conditions were made known to the chief instructor, the problem was easily solved.

Well . . . no. The collection of words that led you to this page is a piece of a course description—and not a very good description, at that. Look at it again:

Discusses and illustrates principles and techniques of computer programming.

Notice that the statement seems to be talking about what the course or the instructor will be doing. There isn't a word about what the student will be able to do as a result of the instruction. I hope you are not being misled by the fact that college catalogs are full of statements like this one. They are *not* statements of learning outcomes, and they are not what we are concerned with here.

Let me try to explain the difference this way. A course description outlines various aspects of a *process* known as instruction. A course objective, on the other hand, is a description of the intended *results* of the instructional process. It's sort of like the difference between bread and baking. Baking is what you do to get the bread, but it isn't the same as bread. Baking is the process; bread is the result. Similarly, instruction is the process; student competence is the result.

Turn to page 7 and read the material again.

3 | The Qualities of Useful Objectives

Objectives are useful tools in the design, implementation, and evaluation of instruction. They are useful in pointing to the content and procedures that will lead to successful instruction, in helping to manage the instructional process itself, and in helping to prepare the means of finding out whether the instruction has been successful. And with objectives in the hands of students, you are able to eliminate the waste that comes from forcing students to guess at what the important outcomes of the instruction might be.

But what are the qualities of useful objectives? What makes one statement meaningful and another meaningless?

Simply put, a usefully stated objective is one that succeeds in communicating an intended instructional result to the reader. It is useful to the extent that it conveys to others a picture of what a successful learner will be able to do that is *identical to the picture the objective writer had in mind.* And the most useful objective is the one that allows us to make the largest number of decisions relevant to its achievement and measurement. Now, any number of combinations of words and pictures and symbols might be used to express an intended outcome. What you are searching for is that group of words or symbols that will communicate your intent exactly as YOU understand it. For example, if you provide other instructors with an objective and they then teach some students to perform in a manner that *you agree* is consistent with what you had in mind, then you have communicated your objective in a meaningful manner. If, on the other hand, you feel that you "had something more in mind" or that they haven't "grasped the essence" of your intent, then your statement has failed to communicate adequately, regardless of how that statement was worded.

A meaningfully stated objective, then, is one that succeeds in communicating your intent; the best statement is the one that excludes the greatest number of possible meanings *other than* your intent.

Unfortunately, there are many slippery words that are open to a wide range of interpretation. (If you have tried to write more than a few sentences that say what you mean, you know how exasperating those little devils can be.) It isn't that such words aren't useful in everyday conversation. After all, you wouldn't want to be skewered with a "What do you mean by that!" every time you said something like "It's a nice day" or "I really appreciate you" or "I'm fine." But if you use *only* such broad terms (or "fuzzies") when trying to communicate a specific instructional intent, you leave yourself open to *mis*interpretation.

Consider the following phrases in this light:

WORDS OPEN TO MANY INTERPRETATIONS	WORDS OPEN TO FEWER INTERPRETATIONS
to know	to write
to understand	to recite
to *really* understand	to identify
to appreciate	to sort
to *fully* appreciate	to solve
to grasp the significance of	to construct
to enjoy	to build
to believe	to compare
to have faith in	to contrast
to internalize	to smile

What do you mean when you say you want learners to know something? Do you mean you want them to recite, or to solve, or to construct? Just to tell them you want them to "know" tells them little—because the word can mean many different things. Until you say what you mean by "knowing" in terms of what students ought to be able to DO, you have said very little at all. Thus, an objective that communicates best will be one that describes the student's intended performance clearly enough to preclude misinterpretation.

How can you do that? What characteristics might help make an objective communicate and help make it useful? Well, there are several schemes that might be used in stating objectives, but the format described on the following pages is one that is known to work, and it is the one I have found easiest to use.

The format includes three characteristics that help make an objective communicate an intent. These characteristics answer three questions: (1) What should the learner be able to do? (2) Under what conditions do you want the learner to be able to do it? and (3) How well must it be done? The characteristics are these:

1. **Performance.** An objective always says what a learner is expected to be able to *do*; the objective sometimes describes the product or result of the doing.
2. **Conditions.** An objective always describes the important conditions (if any) under which the performance is to occur.
3. **Criterion.** Wherever possible, an objective describes the criterion of acceptable performance by describing how well the learner must perform in order to be considered acceptable.

Though it is not always necessary to include the second characteristic and not always practical to include the third, the more you say about them, the better your objective will communicate. Other characteristics *could* be included in an objective, as well, such as a description of the students for which the objective is intended or a description of the instructional procedure by which the objective will be accomplished. But, though these are important pieces of information in the process of designing instruction, the objective is not the place for them. Why not? Because they clutter up the objective and make it more difficult to read and interpret. The objective needs to be *useful* as well as clear; if you begin to stuff all sorts of things into it, it will fail to serve its purpose. (Thousands upon thousands of such objectives have been written . . . but never used.)

It would also be possible to insist that objectives follow some rigid form or format. (I once visited a school in which teachers were expected to write their objectives on a form printed by the principal. His form had a line printed every two inches down the page, the implication being that every objective was no more than seven inches long and two inches high. Would you be surprised to learn that the teachers were hostile to the idea?) But you are not looking for objectives that are a particular size and shape. You are looking for objectives that are *clear*, that say what you want to say about your instructional intents as concisely as possible. And that is all. So, anybody who says that an objective must be no more than two inches high and seven inches wide or who says an objective must or must not contain certain words should be reminded that the function of an objective is to communicate. If it does, rejoice. If it doesn't, fix it! You don't work on an objective until it matches someone's idea of "good looks"; you work on it until it communicates one of your instructional intents—you write as many objectives as you need to describe ALL instructional results you think are important to accomplish.

The following chapters are intended to help you to do just that.

4 ‖ Performance

The characteristics of a useful objective are these:

1. Performance (what the learner is to be able to do)
2. Conditions (important conditions under which the performance is expected to occur)
3. Criterion (the quality or level of performance that will be considered acceptable)

In this chapter we will investigate the first of these characteristics, that of performance. A performance may be visible, like writing or repairing, or invisible, like adding, solving, or identifying.

Note

During the early sixties we talked about behavior rather than about performance. This turned out to be an unfortunate choice of terms. A number of people were put off by the word, thinking that objectives necessarily had to have something to do with behaviorism or with behaviorists. Not so. Objectives describe performance, or behavior, because an objective is specific rather than broad or general and because performance, or behavior, is what we can be specific about.

A statement of an objective is useful to the extent that it specifies what learners must be able to DO or PERFORM when they demonstrate mastery of the objective. Since you cannot peer into another's mind to determine what knowledge or attitudes might reside therein, you must make guesses or inferences about such internal states. These inferences must be based on what people say and do; they must be based, in other words, on the circumstantial evidence of visible or audible human behavior. Often you can observe a desired instructional outcome directly, as, for example, when you watch someone lay a brick, play a piano, or program a computer. But when you are interested in teaching abstract states such as knowledge or attitudes, you can only know whether you have succeeded by observing students DOING something that represents the meaning of those abstractions.

Thus, the most important and indispensable characteristic of a useful objective is that it *describes the kind of performance* that will be accepted as evidence that the learner has mastered the objective. Whatever else a statement may do, if it doesn't state a performance, it isn't an objective.

For example, consider the following:

To develop a critical understanding of the importance of effective management.

Though this might be an important outcome to achieve, the statement doesn't tell you what a learner will be doing when demonstrating mastery of the objective. What would be your guess? Writing an essay on the importance of management? Answering multiple-choice questions on management? Drafting a budget? Preparing a production schedule? Devising a procedure for hiring competent people?

We don't know. The statement doesn't tell. More, it is unlikely that two people would agree on what the statement means; it is open to too many interpretations. There is yet another problem with the statement—"to develop" implies something the instructor will do rather than something the student is expected to be able to do.

Now try this statement:

Given all available engineering data regarding a proposed product, be able to write a product profile. The profile must describe and define all of the commercial characteristics of the product appropriate to its introduction to the market, including descriptions of at least three major product uses.

Let's ask the question again. What would students be doing when demonstrating mastery of this objective? Why, *writing a product profile,* that's what they would be doing. These words describe a performance, thereby providing everyone with useful information about what the instruction is to accomplish.

The way to write an objective that meets the first requirement, then, is to write a statement describing an instructional intent, and then to modify it until it answers the question—

What is the learner DOING *when demonstrating achievement of the objective?*

Let's apply this test to some examples.
Which of the following statements would you say is stated in performance terms?

Be able to write a news article. **page 27.**

Be able to develop an appreciation of music. **page 29.**

You said "be able to write a news article" is written in performance terms.

Sharp! Keep this up, and you'll fall out of the back of the book before you know it.

Apparently you remembered to apply the key question to the statement. What must people DO to demonstrate mastery of the objective? Why, they must write news articles. You can tell when someone is doing that, and so *writing* qualifies as a performance. You don't know whether the writing must be done by hand or on a machine like the one I am flogging at this moment, but you do know that the main performance of concern is writing. If the instrument of writing is important, that will show up in the *conditions* described in the objective. For the moment, you are content with a performance.

Try another one. Turn to the page referred to beside the statement that contains a performance:

Be able to understand mathematics. **page 35.**

Be able to sew a seam. **page 37.**

You said "be able to develop an appreciation of music" was stated in performance terms. Gadzooks!

Maybe you thought so because you were confusing the importance of the intention with the clarity with which the intention was stated.

Ask the magic question: "What would someone be doing when demonstrating mastery of this goal?" Writing an essay on the meaning of opera? Sighing in ecstasy when listening to Bach? Answering multiple-choice questions on the history of music? Buying records? Stomping feet? The statement doesn't say. It doesn't give us a clue.

Let's consider performance a little more closely.

A performance is described by a *doing* word. If the word describes something you might be able to DO, then it describes a performance. If it only describes something you can BE, then it is not a *doing* word.

Here are some examples of *doing* words (performances):

> running
> solving
> discriminating
> writing

Here are some examples of *being* words (abstractions):

> happy
> understanding
> appreciating

Turn to page 31.

You can see someone *running or writing,* and you can find out directly (that is, with a single behavior) whether a person is able to *solve* a problem or *discriminate* between colors. Therefore those words qualify as performances. But you can't see someone *appreciating* or *understanding,* and so those words do not describe performances; rather, they describe abstract states of being. That is, they describe states of being that can only be inferred from performances. You can find out whether people understand something only by watching them act or by listening to them. You can tell whether they have a certain attitude only by watching them say or do something from which the existence of the attitude may be inferred.

See if you can tell the difference between performances (*doing* words) and abstractions (*being* words). Circle the words below that describe performances:

> stating
> writing
> valuing
> drawing
> listing
> appreciating
> internalizing
> smiling

When you have finished, turn to page 33.

Check your responses with mine. The performances are circled.

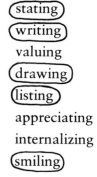

The circled words describe things that people might do. The words not circled describe internal states of being. Valuing, for example, is not something that someone does; rather, it is something that is felt.

Now let's look at some statements and practice recognizing which ones include *performances*. Read the statements below, and turn to the page referred to beside the statement containing a *performance*.

Be able to understand mathematics.   *page 35.*

Be able to sew a seam.   *page 37.*

You said that "be able to understand mathematics" included a performance. Not for a minute.

What would people be *doing* when demonstrating their understanding? Defining mathematics? Writing an essay on Einstein? Solving problems? Correcting problems? Devising problems? The statement doesn't say anything about what someone might be expected to be able to do.

While *understanding* is a fine word for everyday conversation, it is open to far too many interpretations to be useful in an objective.

Try not to be trapped by the fact that the above statement begins with "be able to," as those words can be followed by sheer nonsense. Consider these slippery things:

Be able to develop an increased appreciation and sensitivity.

Be able to internalize a growing awareness.

What would someone be doing when internalizing a growing awareness? What would anyone be doing when developing an appreciation and sensitivity? I dunno. The statement doesn't say.

What we are looking for is the word or words that describe an intended action, whether that action be directly observable (running, writing, editing) or invisible (solving, recognizing, recalling).

Try another one. Turn to the page referred to beside the statement that contains a *performance*:

Be able to apply scientific knowledge. **page 39.**

Be able to stain slides. **page 41.**

There is no reason why an objective must consist of a single sentence. On the contrary, you will find several occasions where quite a few sentences might be required to communicate your intent clearly. This is often true, for example, when you are describing objectives requiring creative activity on the part of the learner. Here is one such example:

> Be able to write a musical composition with a single tonal base within four hours. The composition must be at least sixteen bars long and must contain at least twenty-four notes. You must apply at least three rules of good composition in the development of your score.

Here is another example, this one from a course on human relations:

> Be able to prepare within twenty-four hours analyses of any five of the given case studies. These analyses should discuss the cases according to the principles presented during the course and should describe each problem from the points of view of at least two of the participants. References and notes may be used.

You said "be able to sew a seam" describes performance.

Yes. What are people doing when demonstrating their achievement of this objective? They are sewing something—that's what they are doing. We don't know whether there are any special conditions under which the seam sewing must occur, and we don't know how well someone would have to sew to be considered acceptable, but we do know that they have to sew (or sew it seams). Thus, this statement meets the first requirement of an objective—it includes a performance.

Try another.

Turn to the page referred to beside the statement below that includes a performance:

Be able to apply scientific knowledge.   *page 39.*

Be able to stain slides.   *page 41.*

Well, I suppose I can understand how you might say that "apply scientific knowledge" states a performance. After all, the word *apply* sometimes DOES describe a performance. If the objective were about applying paint or applying makeup to a face, I would agree that I could tell when someone was doing the applying. But "applying scientific knowledge" is rather like "applying oneself with a proper attitude." You don't have the faintest idea of what the student would be doing. Singing a song? Taking out an appendix? Mixing a solution? Constructing a still? The statement doesn't give us any clue.

A statement ought not be called an objective unless, at the very least, it tells us what someone would have to do to demonstrate achievement of the objective. So, when you are looking for the performance, ask the question "What is the *doing* word?"

Turn to page 29, and reread.

Occasionally I hear from someone who is disturbed about the use of the words "be able to."

"I don't want them to be _able_ to do things," goes the complaint, "I want them to DO it. I want to see them doing the things they should be able to do. Therefore, I think it is inappropriate to use those words in an objective."

My reply is that the statement of an objective is supposed to describe a desired capability, that it is supposed to describe something you want the student to be able to do. Therefore, I usually say "be able to" in an objective as a way of communicating that the skill or performance in question should be <u>available on demand.</u> When I want to demand to <u>see</u> that performance, I do so with test items.

Frankly, I don't much care what words you use. If "be able to" pushes you into a psychic trauma, then don't use it. Use whatever words will communicate what you have in mind well enough for others to understand your intents as you understand them.

You said "be able to stain slides" includes a performance. Of course!

You can tell whether the stainer is staining the stainee. Therefore you can tell whether someone is doing what the objective says it is important to be able to do.

One final example. Which of the following statements includes a performance?

Develop a knowledge of food service equipment.   *page 42.*

Be able to add a column of numbers.   *page 43.*

You're putting me on!

How can I help you to internalize your growing awareness of infinite feeling states and consciousness levels if you keep slipping off to pages like these, just to find out what is printed on them?

As long as you're here, though, we might as well share a word or two about the topic at hand. *Develop* is one of those words which by itself doesn't tell you if it is describing a performance. All sorts of things might be developed—theses, neighborhoods, or triceps. But none of these is a performance; none describes anything anyone does. *Develop* is one of those words that depends on the words that follow it for its meaning. Worse, it usually describes instructional *process,* and we want an objective to describe *outcome.*

There are other such sneakies. *Acquiring* an attitude is not at all the same as *acquiring* a wallet. The latter is a performance; the former is not.

Enough of diversion. Let's get back to work.

Turn to page 43.

You said "be able to add a column of numbers" includes a performance. Yes.

What would someone be doing when demonstrating mastery of the objective? Adding a column of numbers. So the statement meets the first requirement of an objective.

OVERT/COVERT

But wait a minute. Something may be a little fishy here. Can you tell whether people are adding? Suppose they were standing perfectly still and claimed to be adding in their heads. Would adding still qualify as a performance?

It would to me, as I consider a performance that which is directly observable or directly assessable. Since I could tell directly whether someone was adding by asking for a *single* written or oral response, I would consider adding a performance. After all, when you are looking for a practical way of writing objectives, it would be awkward to demand that only visible performances be allowed in objectives. As you are often interested in helping students be able to solve problems, recognize specific characteristics, or recall sequences of procedural steps, to exclude these from your objectives would be too much of a distortion to be practical.

Should you be a bit boggled by the terms *overt* and *covert,* be assured that they are old terms of long standing and are used here because they correctly describe the concepts we are considering. OVERT refers to any kind of performance that can be observed directly, whether that performance be visible or audible. COVERT refers to performance that cannot be observed directly, performance that is mental, invisible, cognitive, or internal. Overt performance can be observed by the eye or ear. Covert performance can be detected only by asking someone to say something or to do something visible.

A performance can be *covert* (mental, internal, invisible, cognitive) as long as there is a *direct way* of determining whether it satisfies the objective. "A *direct way*" means a single behavior that will indicate the covert skill. There is an easy way to handle the matter in stating an objective, a way that helps us avoid arguments about just what ought or ought not to be called a covert performance. Simply follow this rule:

> *Whenever the performance stated in an objective is covert, add an <u>indicator behavior</u> to the objective.*

What that means is this: You want students to be able to add? And adding seems like a covert performance? Then just add an indicator behavior to the objective to show the *one single visible thing* students could do to demonstrate mastery of the objective. For example:

> *Be able to add numbers* (write the solutions) *written in binary notation.*

> *Be able to identify* (underline *or* circle) *misspelled words on a given page of news copy.*

Identifying is a covert skill. You can't see anyone doing it. But you could see a person doing activities that were either associated with the identifying or that were the result of the identifying. So? So, all you would do is add a word or two to your objective to let everyone know what directly visible behavior you would accept as an indicator of the existence of the performance. A little practice will show you how it works.

Below are a few expressions; some describe covert performance, and some describe overt performance. Here is what to do: 1. Place check marks ($\checkmark$) beside the expressions that describe performances you can see or hear. 2. Beside those that describe *covert* performances, write the *simplest* indicator behaviors you can think of that would let you know the covert performances existed. (In other words, what visible thing could you ask someone to do that would tell you whether he or she were performing as you desired?)

Play a piccolo.   _____

Discriminate between normal and abnormal X-rays.   _____

Recall the procedure for making a loan.   _____

Identify transistors on a schematic diagram.   _____

Solve word problems.   _____

When you are ready, turn to page 46.

Play a piccolo.	(directly visible and audible; no ✓ indicator needed or acceptable)
Discriminate between normal and abnormal X-rays.	*Sort X-rays into two piles.*
Recall the procedure for making a loan.	*Describe in writing.*
Identify transistors on a schematic diagram.	*Circle.*
Solve word problems.	*Write the Solutions.*

You don't need an indicator behavior to tell whether someone is playing a piccolo; you can hear and see the performance directly. But how can you tell if someone can discriminate between X-rays showing normal function and those showing that something is amiss (or amister)? Discriminating is a skill, but yos can't see it going on. So you need an indicator to show whether the skill is in good shape. Having someone sort a stack of X-rays into piles of "normal" and "abnormal" would be a simple and direct indicator. That single act would tell you directly whether the discriminating were being done to your satisfaction.

How can you tell whether someone is recalling? It's easy. Have that person tell you what is being recalled, either orally or in writing. That is the most direct way. How about answering a set of multiple-choice questions about the topic being recalled—would that be OK? No. Producing a memory without any aid is not the same as producing a memory with the help of the prompts provided by written choices.

How to tell whether students can identify transistors on a schematic? Have them point to the transistors, have them circle the things, or have them poke their pencils through them. That's all you need.

How about solving word problems? Have them write the solutions. If you are more interested in the *procedure* by which they derive the solution, then ask them to write the procedure.

ALWAYS STATE THE MAIN INTENT

Given a number of completed Form 81s, be able to circle the erroneous entries.

Answer these questions about the above statement:

1. What performance is stated?
2. What is the *main point* of the objective?

By now you have quickly spotted that the performance *stated* is "to circle." And I'm sure you also noted that the main thing the objective wants students to be able to do is to discriminate or to identify errors. That's the main intent of the objective. But it doesn't come right out and say so. In this case the main intent is implied but not stated. Here is another one:

Given the brand names of several products currently available to the cosmetologist, be able to underline those that would be considered safe to use as shampoo.

1. What performance is *stated*?
2. What's the *main intent*?

The performance stated is underlining. That's what it says. But that isn't the main intent, is it? After all, there is no value in teaching cosmetologists to go around underlining brand names. The important outcome is for students to be able to *select* products that are safe to use as shampoo. The underlining is just an indicator behavior by which someone will know that the selecting has been done satisfactorily.

In these examples the main intents, though not stated, were clearly implied; you could tell what *meaningful* outcome was intended by reading the objective. Sometimes you will stumble across objectives ("stumble" is the right word) whose main intent is something of a mystery. When that happens, you would be wise to ask their authors what they had in mind.

But when writing your own objectives, I suggest that you always state the main intent—always state the main performance you feel it is important to achieve. Then, if that performance happens to be covert, add an indicator. That way the objective will more successfully fulfill its function of communicating an instructional intent. And now, get thee to a summary.

FIRST SUMMARY

1. *An instructional objective describes an intended outcome of instruction rather than an instructional procedure.*

2. *An objective always states a performance, describing what the learner will be* DOING *when demonstrating mastery of the objective.*

3. *To prepare an objective describing an instructional intent:*

   a. *Write a statement that describes the main intent or performance you expect of the student.*

   b. *If the performance happens to be covert, add an indicator behavior to the objective by which the main performance can be known. Make the indicator the simplest and most direct one possible.*

5 | Conditions

By the time you have written an objective that identifies the behavior you will expect your learners to exhibit when they have successfully completed your course, you will have written a far less ambiguous objective than many which are in use today. Rather than expecting your students to divine what you might have in mind when you use such ambiguous words as *understand, know,* or *appreciate,* you will have at least revealed what you want them to accomplish. And, no matter how skimpy the statement may be, it will exhibit the most important characteristic of all—*it will be written down.* If it isn't written down, it isn't anything. If it *is* written down, it can be improved. And if it states a performance, it can be called an objective. Therefore, by the time your statement identifies a desired performance, you are more than halfway toward developing a useful objective.

But simply specifying the terminal act may not be enough to prevent your being misunderstood. For example, an objective such as "be able to run the hundred-yard dash" may be stated in enough detail to prevent serious misunderstanding, provided the runners are not tricked by unexpected conditions such as having to run barefoot up a muddy slope. But a statement like "be able to compute a correlation coefficient" is another matter. Though the latter objective does state a performance, the learner can misinterpret its intent in several important ways. What kinds of correlations will the learner be expected to compute? Is it important to follow a specified *procedure,* or will only a correct *solution* be considered important? Will the learner be provided with a list of formulas or be expected to work entirely without references or calculating aids? The answer to each of these questions can make a rather important difference in instructional content and emphasis, in how accurately the learners will be able to direct their efforts, and in the test situations that will be appropriate to the objective.

To state an objective clearly, you will sometimes have to state the conditions you will impose when students are demonstrating their mastery of the objective. Here are some examples:

> Given a problem of the following type . . .
> Given a list of . . .
> Given any reference of the learner's choice . . .
> Given a matrix of intercorrelations . . .
> When provided with a standard set of tools . . .
> Given a properly functioning . . .
> Without the aid of references . . .
> Without the aid of a slide rule . . .
> Without the aid of tools . . .

For example, instead of simply specifying "be able to solve problems in algebra," we could improve the ability of the statement to communicate by wording it something like this:

> *Given a linear algebraic equation with one unknown, be able to solve* (write the solution) *for the unknown without the aid of references, tables, or calculating devices.*

How detailed should you be in your description? Detailed enough to be sure the desired performance would be recognized by another competent person, and detailed enough so that others understand your intent as YOU understand it.

Here are some questions you can ask yourself about your objectives as a guide to your identifying important aspects of the target, or terminal, performances you wish to develop:

1. What will the learner be allowed to use?
2. What will the learner be denied?
3. Under what conditions will you expect the desired performance to occur?
4. Are there any skills that you are specifically NOT trying to develop? Does the objective exclude such skills?

To see if I have made myself clear, look at the objective below, and then turn to the page referred to under the part of the sentence you think tells something about the conditions under which the performance is to occur.

Given a list of factors leading to significant historical events,

page 53

be able to identify (underline) *at least five factors contributing*

page 55

to the Crash of 1929.

At one industrial organization, it became desirable to teach some employees "to be able to read electrical meters." Since several skills are implied by this general statement and since it was desired that learners be able to use the statement of objectives as one means of evaluating their own progress, the final statement contained an objective defining each skill, as follows:

1. Given a meter scale, be able to identify (state) the value indicated by the position of the pointer as accurately as the construction of the meter will allow.

2. Be able to identify (state) the value indicated by the pointer on meter scales that are linear, nonlinear, reversed, or bidirectional.

3. Given a meter with a single scale and a range switch, be able to identify (state) the value indicated by the pointer for each of the ranges shown by the range switch.

4. Given a meter with several scales and a range switch, be able to identify (state) the scale corresponding to each setting of the range switch.

With these objectives, you would have a far more accurate picture of what was expected of you than if you were provided with a statement that simply said "be able to read electrical meters."

You chose "given a list of factors leading to significant historical events" as the words describing the conditions or situation under which the selecting behavior was to occur.

Correct. These words tell you that students will not be expected to choose factors from a library of books or from an essay on history or from their memories. The statement tells them that a list will be provided and that they will be expected to recognize rather than to recall.

Here is another objective. Does it contain words describing the conditions under which the performance is to occur?

Given a list of thirty-five chemical elements, be able to recall (write) *the valences of at least thirty.*

Yes. **Turn to page 57.**

No. **Turn to page 58.**

You said the phrase "be able to identify (*underline*)" describes conditions under which the identifying behavior would be expected to occur. Perhaps you are still thinking of the first characteristic of a useful objective, the one requiring the identification of a performance. If so, I'm glad you remembered it. But I am now asking for words that describe the situation or conditions under which the desired performance will be evaluated. Perhaps it will help if you ask the question "With what or to what is the learner doing whatever it is he or she is doing?"

Return to page 51, and select the other alternative.

You said the statement DOES say something about the conditions under which students will be recalling the valences of elements. Yes. It tells you that they will be given a list of elements. This objective has another interesting feature, so let's look at it again:

> *Given a list of thirty-five chemical elements, be able to recall* (write) *the valences of at least thirty.*

Notice that the statement also tells you something about what kind of behavior will be considered "passing." It tells you that thirty correct out of thirty-five is the definition of *acceptable skill.* (If you suspect that this touches on another characteristic of a clearly stated objective, you are correct again. I will have more to say about this in Chapter 6.)

Now proceed to page 59.

You thought the statement did NOT contain words describing conditions. Let's look at the statement again.

Given a list of thirty-five chemical elements, be able to recall (write) *the valences of at least thirty.*

Clearly, the statement meets the first requirement (performance); it states the main intent (recall) and describes the indicator behavior by which the main intent will be detected (*writing the valences of various elements*). Does the statement also tell you anything about the references the students will be allowed to use or the materials they will be given to work with while they are doing the recalling? It *does,* doesn't it? It tells you the second requirement (conditions)—that students will be given a list of elements to work from.

Return to page 53, and select the correct answer.

USING SAMPLE TEST ITEMS

Sometimes a good way to clarify the conditions under which a performance should occur is simply to add a test item to the objective. This is easy to do and often saves writing baskets full of words. For example, consider the following objective:

Be able to start an intravenous injection in a patient's arm.

This statement already says quite a bit. It tells you that students will be expected to actually start an injection rather than merely talk about doing it or answer multiple-choice questions about the skill. It also says that they will have to perform the skill on real people (a condition under which the performance must occur). What it doesn't say is whether students will have to be able to do this on difficult patients (such as fat ones) or whether they will have to do it under some sort of stress or with special equipment. While those conditions could be written into the objective, it might be easier to add a description of the test that will be used to determine whether the objective has been achieved. Like so:

Using standard equipment, be able to start an intravenous (IV) injection in the arm of a patient. (Test: start an IV on any member of the class within two tries.)

Now you know that the performance must occur under class-room conditions and that no stress conditions will be imposed (except, perhaps, on the hapless "patients"). You also know that the student's performance will have to be demonstrated only once in order to be considered satisfactory, provided that it is done correctly within two tries. It's not nice to make pincushions of each other.

Three more examples:

OBJECTIVE

Be able to identify (mark) statements represented by a Venn diagram.

SAMPLE TEST ITEM

Which of the following statements is represented by the Venn diagram below?
    a. All animals are birds.
    b. Some birds are animals.
    c. All birds are animals.
    d. No birds are animals.

("c" is correct)

I call this a sample test item because there are many other items *of this type* that would also be appropriate for testing the desired performance. When there is only ONE possible test item you could use, you might as well call it a test. But it's no big thing. Call it whatever makes the most sense in your situation. Try a second example:

OBJECTIVE

When asked a question in French, be able to reply with an appropriate sentence.

SAMPLE TEST ITEM

Test Tape 5 asks ten questions in French about common banking transactions. When a question is asked, respond in French with a suitable sentence. Record your response. You will have ten seconds to make each response.

This objective tells you that it wants students to be able to reply orally to spoken questions in French. The item makes it clear that the student will have to respond to spoken questions and that the questions will have to do with completing banking transactions. It also reveals that the performance will be expected to occur under classroom conditions, that the questions will be in conversational speed, and that the responses will have to be composed and delivered within ten seconds of hearing the question. I could have written all that into the objective, of course, but sometimes it is easier simply to leave the objective as is and add a sample test item.

The third example:

Be able to solve simple linear equations in one unknown.

To mathematicians who know the subject there is nothing about this statement that is ambiguous. They know exactly what it means. But what about students just learning about the subject? What kind of equations am I talking about? What will the students be doing when demonstrating their achievement of the objective? The simple way to answer those questions here is to add one or more sample test items. Thus:

OBJECTIVE

Be able to solve simple linear equations in one unknown.

SAMPLE TEST ITEM

Solve for x in the following:
   a. $2 + 4x = 12$
   b. $9x - 3 = 6$

Now we know what we will have to work on and what we will have to do to it.

Let me test your perception. Did I say that you would always add test items to your objectives?

Yes.   **Turn to page 62.**

No.   **Turn to page 63.**

You think I said you should always add test items to objectives? Wh . . . why . . . you really think that *I* would say a thing like *that*?

You are not correct . . . to say the least. What I said was that there are times when the easiest way to make an objective communicate more about the conditions under which the performance should occur is to add a test item to the objective. Not always. Only when it seems an easy way to communicate your intent.

How do you know when to do it and when not to? I wish I had a neat answer for that one. All I can tell you is that when you are drafting objectives and it seems you are getting all tangled up with descriptive phrases, try wondering whether the addition of a sample test item won't help make things clear.

Now make believe you answered the question correctly, and turn to page 63.

If this is your first pass at this page, you deserve the eagle-eye award. I never suggested adding items to all objectives.

You see, when you are looking for the simplest and most practical way to communicate your instructional intents, most of the time you can do that by describing your intent in a sentence or three. Once in a while, when you get all tangled up in your own verbiage, you can snip your way out of the mess by simply stating the desired performance and then adding an item as part of the objective. So much for that.

Now for a little more practice in recognizing *conditions* under which desired performance should occur. Read the following objective and then circle the words that describe relevant conditions.

> *Given a* DC *motor of ten horsepower or less that contains a single malfunction, and given a kit of tools and references, be able to repair the motor. The motor must be repaired within forty-five minutes and must operate to within 5 percent of factory specifications.*

When you have circled the conditions, turn to page 65.

Given a DC *motor of ten horsepower or less that contains a single malfunction, and given a kit of tools and references, be able to repair the motor. The motor must be repaired within forty-five minutes and must operate to within 5 percent of factory specifications.*

The words before the first two commas tell you something about the conditions under which the desired performance must occur. They tell you what it is that students will be handling or manipulating. The second sentence is intended to describe the boundaries of acceptable performance. Such boundaries tell you how rapidly and with what accuracy the work must be completed.

Some might argue that "repaired within forty-five minutes" is a description of a condition under which the performance must be done. They might argue that it describes something about the haste with which the task must be performed. Frankly, it shouldn't matter much whether you call it a condition or a criterion of acceptable performance. *Just be sure to state it* if it is important to the performance. The clarity of the objective counts more than agreement on labels for its parts.

Try another practice item. Underline the *conditions,* and then check your response with mine.

Without references, be able to recall (write) *at least seven patient characteristics to which the therapist should respond, and at least five patient characteristics to which the therapist should withhold response.*

Turn to page 67.

> <u>*Without references,*</u> *be able to recall* (write) *at least seven patient characteristics to which the therapist should respond, and at least five patient characteristics to which the therapist should withhold response.*

About the only special condition mentioned here is "without references." Everything else tells you what the students are to *do* and how well they have to be able to do it.

QUESTION: If the objective doesn't *say* the students can use references, can't you presume that they will have to work without them? Can't you *assume* that "no references" is intended? Isn't it a fair inference? Since I can't tell what is in the mind of the objective writer, I can't tell whether it is a fair inference or not. But when you're writing an objective, why take a chance on having your objective misinterpreted when you don't have to? Why not simply add a few words to say what you mean? Then the reader will know for sure, rather than for maybe.

Turn to page 68.

HOW MANY CONDITIONS?

Should every objective state conditions? How finely should conditions be described?

The answer to these questions is, add enough description to an objective to make it clear to everyone concerned just what you expect from the learner. If what you expect is made clear just by stating the desired performance and the degree of excellence you desire (the criterion), then don't add conditions arbitrarily. How can you tell whether the conditions are defined clearly enough? Give your draft objective to one or two students, and ask them what they think they would have to do to demonstrate their mastery of the objective. If their description matches what you have in mind, then you have done well. If it doesn't, then a little patching here or there is in order. But remember the ironclad rule of objective writing:

If there is disagreement about the meaning, don't argue about it—fix it!

The purpose of the objective is to communicate something to somebody. If that somebody doesn't get the message as intended, don't argue or defend—fix!

For now, you have had enough practice with identifying conditions to have the basic idea. There will be more practice later on to sharpen up your skill, so let's move on to the final characteristic of a useful objective, the criterion of acceptable performance.

SECOND SUMMARY

1. *An instructional objective describes an intended outcome of instruction rather than the process of instruction itself.*

2. *An objective always states a performance describing what the learner will be* DOING *when demonstrating achievement of the objective.*

3. *To prepare an objective:*

   a. *Write a statement that describes the main intent or performance expected of the student.*

   b. *If the performance happens to be covert, add an indicator behavior through which the main intent can be known.*

   c. *Describe relevant or important conditions under which the performance is expected to occur. If it seems useful, add a sample test item. Add as much description as is needed to communicate the intent to others.*

6 | Criterion

Having described what you want students to be able to do, you can increase the communication power of an objective by telling them HOW WELL you want them to be able to do it. You will accomplish this by describing the criterion of acceptable performance. A criterion is the standard by which performance is evaluated, the yardstick by which achievement of the objective is assessed.

If you can specify the acceptable performance for each objective, you will have a standard against which to test your instruction; you will have the means for determining whether your instruction is successful in achieving your instructional intent. If, for example, your best experience and wisdom tell you that you must not consider a student competent until that student can perform within a strict time limit, then you know that you will have to instruct and assist that student until the desired performance level is reached. You would know—and the student would know—the quality of the performance to work for or exceed. What you must try to do, then, is indicate in your objectives what the acceptable performance level will be by adding words that describe the criterion of success.

Before you proceed, however, turn to the page that best describes your feeling at this moment.

Many of the things I teach are intangible and CANNOT be evaluated.   *page 73.*

Show me how to describe a criterion of acceptable performance.   *page 74.*

Occasionally someone asks, "Why bother with objectives? If you have good test items, aren't objectives redundant?"

It is a question that deserves comment.

Perhaps I can clarify the relationship between objectives and test items by rephrasing the question this way: "If you have a ruler with which to measure the dimensions of a building, why do you need a blueprint?" Answer: So that anyone will know whether the completed building looks the way it was intended to look and so that similar buildings can be constructed if desired.

The same is true of objectives. If you only had test items, you wouldn't know what critical characteristics were important to develop, you wouldn't know how to construct new or additional items with which to determine whether the main intent has been achieved, and you wouldn't know how to tell whether students were competent enough to be considered acceptable.

Thus, the objective describes where you are going, while test items are the means by which you find out whether you got there.

Well . . . all right . . . but if you are teaching things that cannot be evaluated, you are in the awkward position of being unable to demonstrate that you are teaching anything at all. The issue here is not whether all important things can be measured or evaluated. The issue is simply whether you can improve the usefulness of an objective by making clear how well the student must be able to perform to be considered acceptable. Sometimes such a criterion is critical, and sometimes it is of little or no importance at all. But adding a criterion to an objective is a way of communicating an important aspect of what it is you want your students to be able to do.

While you're here, I might point out that it is almost always possible to analyze the "intangibles" to the point where they become tangible, and thus open to measurement. There is at least one procedure for doing this, called goal analysis,[1] and I use it whenever I feel that it is important for students to have certain attitudes, motivations, inclinations, and so on. These abstract states or conditions can almost always be analyzed into the important performances that define them. And UNTIL abstract states are analyzed into the performances that define them, you cannot make good decisions about what to do to accomplish those states.

Intangibles are often intangible only because we have been too lazy to think about what it is we want students to be able to do.

Turn to page 74.

---

1. Read *Goal Analysis, Second Edition,* R. F. Mager (David S. Lake Publishers, 1984).

All right, let's look at some of the ways in which you can specify acceptable performance in an objective.

Understand before you begin that you are not looking to specify a *minimum* or *barely tolerable* criterion. You are looking for ways to specify the *desired* criterion. Sometimes that means marginal performance and sometimes it means perfect performance. Sometimes it means that considerable error can be tolerated and sometimes it means that no error can be tolerated. Above all, it means that as a result of consulting your best knowledge, wisdom, and experience YOU say how well a student must be able to perform to be considered acceptable, whether that desired performance be casual or perfect.

And it doesn't take too much thought to realize that what is acceptable in one situation can be totally unacceptable in another. While it might be acceptable for a shipping clerk to tie an occasional knot that slips, I doubt that you would consider that level of performance acceptable from a surgeon. So when the expressions *acceptable performance* or *adequate performance* are used, translate them into *desired performance* and then describe the criterion accordingly.

SPEED

One of the common ways to describe a criterion of acceptable performance is to describe a *time limit* within which a given performance must occur. Such a time limit is often implied when you tell students how long an examination period will be. If the speed of performance is important, however, it is better to be explicit about it; then no one will have to guess at what you have in mind for them to do. When time is of the essence, it is only fair to communicate that criterion to the learner. For example, consider this DD (dumb dialogue):

Instructor: You flunk!
Student: But I ran the hundred-yard dash, like you said.
Instructor: True. But you were too slow.

Student: But you didn't say how fast we had to run.

Instructor: Would I ask you to run if I didn't want you to run *fast*? You should have *known* that speed was important.

If speed is important, say so in the objective, and more people will perform as you intend.

If you do NOT intend to evaluate a performance on the basis of its speed, you need not and *should not* impose a time limit. The rule is to impose only those criteria that are important. If it is important that the running be done to a speed criterion, then the objective might better read:

Be able to run the hundred-yard dash on a dry track within fourteen seconds.

Then everyone would know what they should do, where they should do it, and how fast they should do it.

Let's try a little practice in recognizing criteria stated in an objective. Read the following. Then turn to the page referred to below the words you think describe the criterion of acceptable performance, the words that tell how well the learner must be able to perform the task.

Given five centrifugal pumps, each containing one malfunction, and being told one symptom of each malfunction, be able to locate (describe and point to) *the*

page 77

malfunction. Any tools, instruments, and references may be used. Four of five malfunctions must be located within ten minutes each.

page 78

Perhaps you have had academic experiences similar to this one. During class periods of a seventh-grade algebra course, a teacher provided a good deal of skillful guidance in the solution of simple equations and made sure that all students had enough practice to give them confidence in their ability. When it came time for an examination, however, the test items consisted mainly of stated (word) problems, and the students performed rather poorly. The teacher's justification for this "sleight of test" was that the students didn't "really understand" algebra if they could not solve word problems.

Perhaps the teacher was right. But the skill of solving equations is considerably different from the skill of solving word problems; if he wanted his students to learn how to solve word problems, he should have taught them how to do so.

Don't expect a learner to be able to exhibit Skill B simply because you have given practice in Skill A.

You think that "be able to locate *(describe and point to)*" describes a criterion of acceptable performance. No. I think you may still be thinking about performance rather than quality of performance. While I'm glad you remembered this key characteristic of an objective, the words you selected tell WHAT the learner is to be able to do rather than HOW WELL it is to be done.

I suppose one could argue that a criterion is *implied* in the words you selected. "The objective says it wants people to be able to point to malfunctions. That's all that was intended," one might say. True, but then the statement goes on to say something very clearly about how well the pointing is supposed to occur. Let's not rely on implications when explications are present—or easily added.

When looking for words describing the criterion of acceptable performance, look for the answer to the question "How *well* does the learner need to perform to have mastered the objective?"

Turn to page 75, and read the item again.

You said "four of five malfunctions must be located within ten minutes each" is the criterion. You've got it.

You can see that in this case students will be locating malfunctions in centrifugal pumps. That's the main intent of the objective. How well must they perform to be considered acceptable? Well, each student will be given five pumps, each with a malfunction, and the student will have to locate four of the five malfunctions, locating each within ten minutes. Those who can't find that many within that period of time aren't yet good enough at that skill.

"Where did the ten minutes come from?" you may ask. Why not twelve minutes or half an hour? Because the objective writer decided that if students can do it in ten minutes, at the end of instruction they will be prepared to do whatever comes next—learn a more complex or advanced task, begin repairing pumps, or perhaps supervise other pump repairers. Sometimes the criterion decision is wholly arbitrary (in which case it is *super* important to tell students what it is, as they are unlikely to guess what that criterion might be). Often the criterion is set by answering these questions:

1. How well must a student be able to perform in order for practice to be the only requirement for improvement?

2. How competent must the student be in order to be ready for the next assignment (the next objective, the next course, the job itself)?

Set the criterion as best you can, and then adjust it on the basis of what is reasonable.

ACCURACY

Speed is only one way to determine a criterion of success. Sometimes the accuracy of a performance is more important than its speed, and sometimes both speed and accuracy are important.

Here's an example of accuracy:

Be able to state the time shown on the face of any clock to within one minute of accuracy.

Since the rapidity of the performance is unimportant, no speed criterion is shown.

Or, your objective might include criteria like these:

. . . and solutions must be accurate to the nearest whole number.

. . . with materials weighed accurately to the nearest gram.

. . . correct to at least three significant figures.

. . . with no more than two incorrect entries for every ten pages of log.

. . . with the listening accurate enough so that no more than one request for repeated information is made for each customer contact.

Use whatever words or means will communicate how well your students must perform before you will be willing to certify them as competent.

Try this example:

Given a compass, ruler, and paper,

page 80

be able to construct and bisect *any given angle larger than five*

page 81

degrees. *Bisections must be accurate to one degree.*

page 83

Turn to the page indicated beneath the words that describe the criterion of acceptable performance.

Yoiks! You said that "given a compass, ruler, and paper," was a criterion of acceptable performance. How *could* you!

Look at the words again, and answer the question "How well must the angle bisecting be done if the student is to be considered adequate?" Do those words tell you the answer? No, they don't. They tell you what the student is going to have to work with when performing as desired.

Honestly, now, why did you turn to this page?

I really thought it was the correct response.   **page 79.**

Aw, I just wanted to see what you'd say.   **page 83.**

You said, "be able to construct and bisect" describes a criterion.

No, those words describe the performance. They tell you what the learner is expected to be able to *do*, but they don't tell you how well it would have to be done. When looking for words describing criteria, ask yourself questions such as these:

- How well must the student be able to perform?
- How will I know when the student is competent enough to be certified as having accomplished the objective?

Turn to page 79, and take another look.

Let's split a hair.

As you work with objectives you will come to notice that while the performances stated therein tell you what people are expected to be able to DO, the criteria often may describe the characteristics (or shapes) of the PRODUCTS of that doing. When, for example, objectives ask that someone be able to:

- write a report
- construct an amplifier
- repair a word processor

the criteria will describe the desired characteristics of the end products of those performances. The criteria will say something about the characteristics of the final report, the completed amplifier, or the repaired word processor, rather than about how those products were produced (the shapes of the performances).

"So what?" I hear you muttering. So not a whole lot. It's just that in these instances you determine whether the performance is adequate by looking at the product of the performance rather than at the performance itself. And you make darn sure you don't allow people to be evaluated on the shape of their performance when it is the shape of the product that is important. Don't allow the sort of evaluation that says, "Oh sure, her report is terrific in all respects, but she wrinkles her nose when she types so we'll have to take ten points off."

It's "nice to know" the distinction between performance and its product, because sometimes your criteria will need to describe performance or product, and sometimes some of both. But, your attention should be directed toward describing the criteria that matter, regardless of their labels.

You said "bisections must be accurate to one degree" are the words describing the criterion of success.

That's exactly right. These are the words by which you will be able to tell when to certify the student as having accomplished the objective.

QUALITY

Many times the speed and/or accuracy of a performance are not the critical criteria. Instead, something about the quality of the performance must be present if the performance is to be considered acceptable. For example, one of the skills that missile maintenance people must develop has to do with the adjustment of a round TV screen called a PPI. On the face of this screen is a round range marker that is electronically produced; one thing the maintenance folks must do is adjust this circle until it is *round*. But how round? What is round enough? You can see that it doesn't help much merely to tell people that it has to be <u>very round</u>. And it certainly doesn't help to underline the words. While underlining or italics might emphasize the importance of the roundness, they say nothing about the required degree of the roundness.

How to communicate the desired quality of the performance? One way would be to define the amount of *acceptable deviation* from perfection or from some other standard. You could put a round template on the screen and tell the students that their range marker will be round enough when no part of it deviates more than one-eighth inch from the standard. The objective might look something like this:

> *Given a properly operating XX-1 missile system and a standard kit of tools, be able to adjust the PPI range marker to acceptable roundness within forty-five seconds. Acceptable roundness: no more than one-eighth inch deviation from a standard template.*

Notice that in this case quality *and* speed of performance are important. It wouldn't do to diddle around with the PPI scope for long periods of time. There might be dire consequences.

Another example of a quality criterion may be found in the workshop that Peter Pipe and I developed to help people learn how to design and implement criterion-referenced instruction (CRI).[2] One module requires participants to be able to speak "coherently" about criterion-referenced instruction. But what does coherently mean in this context? Well, it means they need to be able to speak clearly and accurately. Oh yeah? And what does *that* mean? You can see that a better definition of the criterion is in order. We wrote the objective this way:

> *Given access to any sources available, be able to prepare and present a videotaped talk intended to inform a group of your superiors, colleagues, or the public of the merits of criterion-referenced instruction. You are expected to specify the group to which your talk is directed. The talk will:*
>
> - *describe at least five characteristics in which CRI differs from conventional instruction,*
> - *anticipate at least three common misconceptions about CRI and offer suitable rebuttals, and*
> - *describe at least two benefits that might accrue to your specified audience from the use of CRI.*
>
> *The talk should last not more than ten minutes.*

Now you know a great deal more about the expected performance than you did when you were told only that you had to prepare and present a coherent talk. Participants in the workshop can—and often do—include considerably more in their videotapes than the requirements given above. But the evaluation of the videotapes is carefully confined to the criteria defined in the objective. It would be grossly dishonest for us to do otherwise (e.g., "Sure, you included all the requirements for a successful videotape, but you didn't smile often enough, so we will have to take ten points off for poor attitude").

---

2. *CRI (Criterion-Referenced Instruction): Analysis, Design, and Implementation, Second Edition,* an individualized workshop by R. F. Mager and Peter Pipe (Mager Associates, Carefree, Arizona, 1983).

POINTING TO THE CRITERION

There are at least three ways to indicate a criterion without actually describing the criterion in the objective. All are ways of *pointing* to the criterion:

1. If an intended criterion has been made *explicit* in some document or other, the simple thing to do in the objective is to add words that tell where to find the criterion. For example:

   ... according to the Standards Chart, 1984 edition.

   ... Criterion: manufacturer's specifications, *Repair Manual, Corrugated Soap,* 1997 edition.

   ... according to the criteria described on p. 33, *Manual 27-10.*

This procedure should be used, however, only when the criterion is clearly stated in the reference you are pointing to and only when that reference is always available to both students and instructors.

2. If the desired performance consists of a number of steps, and if an evaluation checklist exists, you might point to that checklist as a description (or partial description) of the criterion. For example:

   ... Criterion: all steps to be performed as well as, and in the sequence described by, the Cheeky Checklist of Proper Kissing.

   ... with each action to compare in quality (sequence is not important) with the Performance Checklist of Turgid Terpsichore.

3. On rare occasions you might find it appropriate to point to competent performance shown on a piece of film or videotape, saying, in effect, "Do it like *that.*" This might be useful if the performance involves complex movements difficult to describe, such as dance steps, diving, or underwater maneuvers. I hesitate to mention this method, however, for fear that someone will take it as a license to use *only* a film or videotape

without also describing the key characteristics of the desired performance in the objective itself. Such a practice would be almost as uninformative as that other false criterion, "to the satisfaction of the instructor." Refer to film, videotape, or documents only if they help in making the desired criterion clear to all concerned.

CONDITION OR CRITERION?

Sometimes it is not easy to read an objective and tell whether a phrase describes a condition or a criterion. Sometimes the two rather blend together. For example:

Be able to do consecutively thirty push-ups, thirty sit-ups, and ten pull-ups without the use of mechanical aids.

What is the criterion? The *number* of acts that must be performed? Possibly, but some would read that as part of the conditions. Some would say that "without the use of mechanical aids" also is part of the criterion. Their argument would go this way: A criterion tells how good a performance must be, and in this case the performance must be good enough to be done without aids. Who is right?

Not a question worth arguing about. What is important is that an objective be refined until it communicates the intent of the writer. If it answers the following questions, I would consider it a useful objective, regardless of whether everyone agreed on the labels for the phrases:

- What is the main intent of the objective?
- What does the learner have to do to demonstrate achievement of the objective?
- What will the learner have to do it with or to? And what, if anything, will the learner have to do without?
- How will we know when the performance is good enough to be considered acceptable?

If you cannot specify a criterion with as much clarity as you would like, this should not prevent you from trying to communicate as completely as you can with the learner and with colleagues. Certainly, you should be able to find *some* way to evaluate anything you think important enough to spend a significant amount of time teaching. If you cannot, perhaps you should review the alleged importance of teaching it.

THIRD SUMMARY

1. *An objective is a collection of words, symbols, and/or pictures describing one of your important intents.*

2. *An objective will communicate your intent to the degree you describe what the learner will be* DOING *when demonstrating achievement of the objective, the important conditions of the doing, and the criterion by which achievement will be judged.*

3. *To prepare a useful objective, continue to modify a draft until these questions are answered:*

   • *What do I want students to be able to do?*

   • *What are the important conditions or constraints under which I want them to perform?*

   • *How well must students perform for me to be satisfied?*

4. *Write a separate statement for each important outcome or intent; write as many as you need to communicate your intents.*

5. *If you give your written objectives to your students, you may not have to do much else.*

   Why? Because often students are already able to do what you are asking them to do and will be happy to demonstrate their ability, now that they know what is wanted of them.

7 | Pitfalls and Barnacles

Over the past two decades or so, those of us who have been concerned with systematic instructional design have seen many ways in which objectives have been used—and misused. We have seen the most ludicrous statements identified as objectives, we have seen statements with confusing phrasing or useless words, and we have seen profound-sounding statements that couldn't help anyone at all. On the other hand, we have seen well-stated objectives used to assist both the instructor and the student in accomplishing mutually desired ends. In short, we have seen objectives used to assist in instruction, we have seen many that could only impede instruction, and —possibly worst of all—we have seen objectives written with great thought and labor that were never used at all.

Therefore, in this chapter I would like to offer you some of the fruits of our experience by pointing to common problems in the preparation of objectives. Perhaps by pointing to some of the pitfalls I will help you to avoid them.

FALSE PERFORMANCE

This point was made earlier, but its importance makes it warrant some repetition. One of the most pervasive defects of statements that are mistakenly called objectives is that they have the appearance of objectives but contain no performances; they are not objectives at all. Here are some examples:

Have a thorough understanding of particle physics.
Demonstrate a comprehension of the short-story form.
Be able to relate to others in a demonstration of empathy.
Be able to think critically and analytically.
Be able to understand individual differences in patients.

Expressions such as these lead to statements that may describe some important goals in very broad terms. But they are not objectives as they do not say what someone would have to do to demonstrate mastery of the intent.

When statements without performances are thought of as objectives, they lead to a variety of confusions. People are likely to argue about which instructional procedure is suitable for accomplishing the vaguely stated intent and are frustrated when the statement offers no firm guidelines. They cannot agree on methods for assessing achievement of the intent and may complain that all objectives are useless. *They* are at a loss to understand why their *students* are at a loss to understand what they are expected to be able to do. Little wonder, as broad statements provide few clues to action.

When interpreting or drafting an objective, the first step is to look for the performance. Draw a circle around it. If there isn't a performance to draw a circle around, it isn't an objective . . . yet. Fix it, or forget it.

FALSE GIVENS

Another common error (error in the sense that it does not help in communicating an instructional intent) is the inclusion of false givens. These are words or phrases that may follow the word *given* in an objective but that describe something *other* than specific conditions the learner must have or be denied when demonstrating achievement of the objective. Most typically, the words describe something about the instruction itself, such as the following:

Given three days of instruction on . . .
Given that the student has completed six laboratory experiments on . . .
Given that the student is in the category of gifted . . .
Given adequate practice in . . .

As indicated earlier, an objective is useful to the degree that it communicates an intended outcome. If you allow it to describe instructional procedure, you will restrict all concerned in using their best wisdom and experience to help accomplish that outcome. Make sure that the conditions described in your objectives tell something about the situation in which you expect the student to demonstrate competence.

TEACHING POINTS

Related to the false givens is the error of writing an objective to describe a teaching point, a practice exercise, or some other aspect of classroom activity. For example, consider this:

Be able to choose an art print or photo that illustrates a theme of your choice and explain how it illustrates that theme.

Why would you want a student to do such a thing? Certainly it isn't because a meaningful thing to do in the world is to go around explaining to people the theme that's illustrated by a photo you have chosen. Presumably, the reason for wanting students to engage in this activity is that it will help them learn to do something that *can* be considered a meaningful skill. The argument is not with the usefulness of having students practice selecting prints and explaining themes; the argument is with writing descriptions of such activities and calling them objectives. For two practical reasons: The first is that if you describe all instructional activities or teaching points and call them objectives, you will be up to your . . . er . . . a . . . well, you'll be drowning in verbiage. (This is one reason some teachers complain that there are too many objectives.) The second reason is that the main function of an objective is to help course planners decide on instructional content and procedure. If the objective describes a teaching procedure, it will fail to perform its primary purpose because it will be describing instructional practice rather than important instructional outcomes.

This problem can be avoided by asking each draft objective *why* you want students to be able to do what you've described. If your answer is "Because *that* is one of the things they need to be able to do," then the objective probably ought to stand. If,

however, your answer is "So that they will be able to___,"
and you fill in the blank with something *other* than what the
draft objective describes, then that draft objective may describe
a teaching procedure and should be modified so it describes the
desired outcome, instead. Here is another example:

> *Be able to discuss in class the case histories handed out by*
> *the instructor.*

Why did this instructor want students to be able to discuss
written case histories in class? Her answer was something like
this: "Because if they are going to be able to solve problems,
they need to be able to tell the difference between statements of
fact and statements of opinion. The discussion of case histories
gives them practice in doing that." Ah so. Her response made it
clear that her original objective described a teaching procedure
rather than an intended outcome, a means rather than an end.
She would find this objective more useful, therefore, if she
modified it to describe the meaningful skill that was the *reason*
for the practice activity of case discussions:

> *Given written descriptions of problem situations involving*
> *interactions, be able to identify* (label) *statements of fact*
> *and statements of opinion.*

Write your objectives about meaningful skills, and you will
avoid drowning in trivial sentences.

JIBBERISH

A problem similar to that of the false performance is that
sometimes the so-called objectives either contain, or are composed entirely of, words with little or no meaning. The following are examples of worthless expressions:

> Manifest an increasing comprehensive understanding . . .
>
> Demonstrate a thorough comprehension . . .
>
> Relate and foster with multiple approaches . . .
>
> Have a deep awareness and thorough humanizing grasp . . .

When such words are followed by a description of desired performance, they are not disastrous; they just get in the way. If they are not so followed, the danger is more substantial. The danger is that people will be lulled into thinking something meaningful has been said and then may question their own sanity or intelligence because they fail to perceive the meaning that isn't there. For example, "demonstrate the ability to make practical application of information in a creative way." What in the world would someone be doing when demonstrating mastery of such a fogged intent? When you see an entire statement like that, which consists of a meaningless combination of words and symbols, you can understand why some people complain that objectives are useless.

> *Embark on a lifelong search for truth, with the willingness and ability to pose questions, examine experience, and construct explanations and meanings.*

> *Each gifted child will exhibit intellectual growth through the use of each level of the cognitive domain—i.e., knowledge, comprehension, analysis, synthesis, and evaluation—as documented on the district evaluation form.*

> *The student must be able to demonstrate an ability to develop self-confidence and self-respect.*

Verbiage such as this may seem impressive, but it is of little use in communicating instructional intents. Nor can I offer an improved version of these statements, as I don't know what their writers were trying to convey. Fortunately, there is a simple solution.

The best way I know of dejibberizing an objective is to give it to one or two students and ask them what they think it means. While their utterances may sometimes be a little hard on the ego, those utterances will usually show the way toward a cleaner, simpler statement of your intent.

And don't forget editors. A good editor can make miraculous moves toward simplicity and clarity by changing just a few words here and there, and I am continually amazed at how helpful they can be. (You have to watch them, though, for many are slaves to their style manuals and are sometimes willing to sacrifice meaning in their push for conformity. They should periodically be smote smartly about the head and shoulders with a rolled style manual to help them remember their proper place.)

INSTRUCTOR PERFORMANCE

Another practice that interferes with the usefulness of an objective is that of describing what the instructor is expected to do rather than what the student is expected to be able to do:

> *The teacher will provide an atmosphere that will promote the development of self-esteem, confidence, and security in students.*

> *The teacher will help the student recognize natural consequences of behavior.*

> *The instructor will assist the student in the development of . . .*

> *Demonstrate to students the proper procedures for completing Form 321.*

> *Develop in the student . . .*

Phrases such as these might properly describe an instructor objective or an administrative objective, but they say nothing about what results are to be expected insofar as student competence is concerned. Similarly, statements that begin:

> *Each student will . . .*

> *Eighty percent of the students will . . .*

have no meaning whatever to a student, either. What can a student do about an "objective" that says "70 percent of the students must be able to demonstrate an ability to read"? Such statements may provide the basis for instructor objectives, but they are of no help to students.

An instructional objective describes student performance; it avoids saying anything about instructor performance. To do otherwise would unnecessarily restrict individual instructors from using their best wisdom and skills to accomplish the objective.

When reviewing your draft objective, ask it whether it is talking about student performance. If so, rejoice; if not, revise.

FALSE CRITERIA

A more insidious defect is to state a "criterion" that tells the students little or nothing that they don't already know. Consider these:

To the satisfaction of the instructor.

Must be able to make 80 percent on a multiple-choice exam.

Must pass a final exam.

Students know they have to satisfy the instructor. What *would* be news would be to tell them just what they would have to *do* to produce such satisfaction. If an instructor *does*, in fact, make judgments about whether students are or are not competent, there is no reason why those instructors cannot say something about the basis for their judgments. Of course, it might take some thought and effort. So what? That's what professional instruction is all about.

The second and third examples above tell the student a little something about the administrative aspects of the criterion situation but tell them nothing about how well they will have to do whatever the objective demands. To say "80 percent on a multiple-choice exam" is not to describe the desired quality of performance. We all know how easy it is to manipulate the difficulty of an examination by varying the wording and the choice of items. Note that the 80 percent isn't the problem; it is the substance of the 80 percent that is the problem. If you were told, for example, that you were expected to be able to shoot well enough so that 80 percent of your shots fell within the bull's-eye, you would have a description of competence level that you could do something about. To say that you had to get 80 percent on a multiple-choice exam or 90 percent on an essay exam, or to say that you had to reach an 80/90 criterion, is to tell you little that could help you to guide your own efforts. The same is true for the designer of the instruction—such "criteria" do not help in deciding the type and amount of instruction called for in accomplishment of the objective.

If you want to see how bad things can get, read the following, which warrants exposure but not comment:

> *Given twenty problems dealing with three operations in decimals and two types of percent and percentage problems; 90 percent of the students whose chronological ages range from 11.0 to 11.11 and who have given evidence, by the Lorge-Thorndike or other ability test, that they will achieve above the third quartile, will solve the problems and write the solutions at 92 percent accuracy as evidenced by scores on a teacher-devised test administered by May!!!!*

To test the criterion in an objective, ask whether the criterion (1) says something about the quality of performance you desire, (2) says something about the quality of the *individual* performance rather than the group performance, and (3) says something about a real, rather than an imaginary, standard.

RELATED ISSUES

Five issues remain on which I should like to comment. They don't have to do with the actual wording of objectives, so they do not fall strictly within the limits of this book. But since they do constitute common problems relating to objectives, I think they deserve a mention.

Irrelevant Test Items

A common practice is that of testing for achievement of an objective with test items that have little or nothing to do with the performance called for by the objective. For example, though an objective may make it clear that students need to be able to <u>write</u> sonnets, the test items might very well look like these:

1. Define *sonnet*.
2. Name three great sonnet writers.
3. Write a short essay emphasizing the place of the sonnet in eighteenth-century life.

It is clear that defining sonnets is not at all the same as writing them. Neither is naming writers or writing essays the same as writing sonnets.

Common rationalizations for this highly questionable practice of testing with irrelevant items include:

They can't write a sonnet if they don't know what one is.

They can't really appreciate sonnets unless they know something about them.

But I like to vary the type of items I use so as to make my tests interesting.

I'm teaching for transfer.

I want my tests to be a learning situation.

I have to design tests so they can be machine scored.

Students should learn by discovery.

Regardless of the excuse, the use of irrelevant test items in assessing achievement of an objective poses several dangers. For one thing, it models deceit for the students. It tells them that it doesn't bother the instructor to teach one thing and then test for something else. For another thing, the practice is dangerous to the extent that accomplishment of the objective is important. If achieving the objective will have a significant consequence, then it is important to find out whether the objective has been achieved as desired. With irrelevant test items it is impossible to determine that; with irrelevant test items you will never know whether the student has learned to perform as desired. A well-written objective will dictate the form of the test items by which the objective can be assessed.[1]

Wrong Objectives

When you hear the charge that certain objectives are trivial, there are generally two underlying problems to check for, neither of which has to do with the wording of the objective itself. For one thing, you cannot tell whether an objective is a candidate for the charge of triviality without comparing the purpose of the objective with the world around it. That is, you can't tell whether an objective is trivial merely by reading it—you must first determine the *consequence* of achieving or not achieving it. If it wouldn't matter to anybody or anything whether the objective were achieved, then it is a candidate for the charge of triviality. If, on the other hand, some significant consequence would result if the objective were or were not accomplished, then it is not trivial, regardless of how simply it may be worded. Suppose, for example, one objective for a bank teller says, "Be able to smile visibly when serving a customer." That sounds rather trivial if you only read the words. But suppose you know for a fact that unsmiling tellers lose customers? There's nothing trivial about going bankrupt—or about losing a job.

As I said, there are two main reasons for the charge of triviality. One is that the objectives in question are, in fact, trivial. The second is that the objective in question describes something *less than*—something *subordinate to*—the main, or terminal, performance desired. For example, people who are learning to perform appendectomies must first be able to do

---

1. For practice in the skill of developing items relevant to an objective, see *Measuring Instructional Results, Second Edition,* R. F. Mager (David S. Lake Publishers, 1984).

other tasks: decide where to cut, select appropriate instruments, use those instruments, tie knots, and so on. Each of these skills is subordinate or prerequisite to the main skill of performing the appendectomy. If objectives are written *only* to describe subordinate skills and *not* the main, or terminal, skills, they may very well evoke either a charge of triviality or a charge that there are too many objectives.

To avoid such problems, try working both ways against the middle:

First, after drafting an objective, ask yourself why you want someone to be able to do *that*. Draft an objective to describe your answer(s), and then ask yourself why you want someone to be able to do *that*. This procedure will help you to identify the real reason why you are instructing in the first place. Thus: We want our students to be able to recognize dangling participles. What in the world for? Why, so they can recognize well-written sentences. Oh, and why should they be able to do that? Well, so they will be able to *write* well-written sentences. And why should they be able to do that? Well, so they can prepare reports. And why should they be able to prepare reports? Well, because that is one of the tasks they will have to perform. Oh ho! So something that may look trivial by itself (recognizing dangling participles) turns out to be a skill subordinate to that of being able to write reports. Show how your subordinate objectives are tied to the larger, more meaningful skills, and you will be more likely to avoid the charge of triviality (where that charge is unwarranted).

Second, after drafting an objective, ask yourself what someone would need to know or be able to do in order to practice the performance stated in the objective. This will help you to locate the subordinate skills that students will have to have if they are to be ready to tackle the total skill. Thus: What would students have to be able to do before they could start practicing their appendectomies? Well, they would have to be able to tie knots with surgical thread, for one thing. Aha! There is a subordinate skill. Since it is a meaningful skill all by itself, you might write an objective to describe it. What else?

*Here is an example of a skill hierarchy, or pyramid, showing the relationships between the skills involved in making a pizza.**

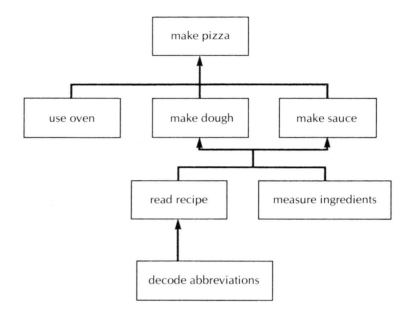

Read the hierarchy this way: Before students can practice the main skill (making pizza), they need to be able to use an oven, make dough, and make sauce. These skills are subordinate (prerequisite) to the terminal skill in that they must all be learned before the terminal skill can be practiced in its entirety. But these three skills are independent of one another; they can be learned in any order.

Before the skills of making dough or making sauce can be practiced, students will have to be able to read a recipe and measure ingredients. These skills are both subordinate to the sauce- and dough-making but are independent of one another. Either could be learned first. Finally, to read a recipe, the learner first has to learn how to decode abbreviations.

---

*Hierarchy courtesy of Diane Pope.

Well, they would have to be able to recognize a scalpel when they see one and be able to ask for it by name. Aha, again. But since scalpel recognizing is only one step, or one part of a meaningful skill, you would not write an objective about it. You would include it in a unit of instruction designed to teach the meaningful skill, but it wouldn't warrant an objective by itself. And when you write objectives about the meaningful skills and not about the steps of those skills, you will avoid being overwhelmed by objectives and will avoid having your objectives called trivial.

False Taxonomizing

A taxonomy is a way of classifying things according to their relationships. If you have never heard the term before, you should skip this section, as it does not describe a problem that relates to you. You won't miss a thing.

Every now and again we bump into someone who claims to be having unusual difficulty in drafting objectives. They feel their objectives are unsatisfactory, even though review of their work reveals objectives that are quite well stated. Then, why the discomfort? Taxonomitis. For some reason these troubled souls are trying to distort their objectives to fit some sort of taxonomy (classification system). Just because it is *possible* to write objectives that reflect different levels of a classification scheme, they seem to feel it is therefore *necessary* to do so. "All our objectives are at the same taxonomy level," they complain. "We need some at other levels," they assert. One person even felt that objectives had to conform to a normal distribution of classification levels to be considered satisfactory. What in the world for? I don't know where such an idea originated, but I wish it would go away.

If you have said what you want your students to be able to do, you have said what they should be able to do. And if those objectives have been derived out of a suitable analysis or out of your best wisdom and experience, what more do you need? Why change the objective just to conform to a taxonomy?

Now, a taxonomy, or classification scheme, can be useful in reminding you of the range of objectives you might write or select, the words you might use in describing your intents, or the kinds of test items that might be appropriate for assessing your objectives. But to deliberately write objectives to fit a classification system rather than a *need* seems a gross misuse of these thinking tools.

Orphan Objectives

One of the strangest and most wasteful practices in relation to objectives is that of writing some and then putting them on the shelf—unused. People who engage in this ritual then complain bitterly that objective writing is a waste of time. And for them it is. If they don't know what to do with objectives once they've got them, or if they don't intend to find out what to do with them, then they are clearly wasting their time in writing objectives.

Why would anyone write objectives who didn't intend to do something with them? Mostly because some well-meaning administrator ordered them to. But to order people to write objectives without first teaching them *how,* or *why,* is to invite dissension and frustration. After all, drafting objectives is only one of a series of steps in the analysis, design, and implementation of instruction. To order that it be carried out in a vacuum is a wasteful practice; at the very least, it will produce objectives that do little more than gather dust.

"Attitude" Objectives

Sometimes you will see statements like the following:

Have a favorable attitude toward reading.

Develop a positive attitude toward numbers.

Have an appreciation for literature.

Have a sense of personal responsibility.

Where is the performance? There isn't any. Therefore they aren't objectives. They are not specific descriptions of intent.

Statements like these describe *states of being;* they do not describe *doing.* While such statements may address areas of extreme importance, it is misleading to refer to them as "attitude" or "affective" objectives.

What is misleading about it is that the readers of such statements may be lulled into thinking they have read objectives merely because the topics are important, and objective writers may be lulled into thinking that when they have written such statements, they have finished their work. On the contrary, they have just begun. You see, statements about the affective (feeling, attitude) are *always* statements of *inference,* not of performance. They are statements about *being* that are inferred from the circumstantial evidence of what people say and do. Thus if you see me stuffing myself with popcorn, you might say that I have a favorable attitude toward popcorn. You may or may not be correct, but the behavior is the only basis you have for the inference.

How, then, can we describe our affective and other abstract intentions in the form of objectives? First, define the intent in terms of the performances that would satisfy you that the intent had been achieved. Then write objectives to describe those performances that represent meaningful skills. (One procedure for this is called goal analysis,[2] a procedure that any objective writer would find useful. It is a procedure to call upon whenever you have abstract intentions you believe worthy of accomplishment.)

Here is a quick example: A manager was concerned that employees "be safety conscious." But what did that mean? How would an employee have to perform to be considered acceptably safety conscious? Clearly, it was mandatory to say what the term meant before good decisions could be made for accomplishing the goal. A goal analysis revealed that it meant, among other things, that he wanted employees to wear safety equipment, follow safety rules, and report safety hazards.

---

2. *Goal Analysis, Second Edition,* R. F. Mager (David S. Lake Publishers, 1984).

Those were all performances, and an objective was written to describe each skill. Collectively, the objectives said what that manager meant by safety consciousness. Note, however, that the objectives were written to describe the performances rather than the abstract state (safety consciousness) they defined.

Whenever you find yourself wanting to write objectives to describe states or conditions that are essentially abstract (understanding, attitude, motivation, feeling), first use goal analysis or any similar procedure to help you define those goals in terms of the performance(s) that would represent their accomplishment. Then you can write objectives to describe those performances you will need to teach.

A checklist you'll find in Chapter 8 can help you review your draft objectives to avoid the pitfalls. But try not to make a big thing out of form and format. The point is to communicate your intent. Say what you want your students to be able to do, what they will be doing it to or doing it without, and how well they will have to do it for you to consider them competent. That's all that objective writing is about.

And now, what's your pleasure?

A little more practice wouldn't hurt.   **Turn to Chapter 8, p. 105.**

I'm ready to test my skill.   **Turn to Chapter 9, p. 123.**

8 || Sharpen Your Skill

The old adage about practice making perfect has about as much and as little truth in it as the one about experience being the best teacher. Practice will improve a skill, and experience will help one's competence—but *only* if there is feedback regarding the quality of the performance. If you don't find out how well you are doing while you are practicing or experiencing, your skill is not likely to improve. Therefore, while practice is important, practice with feedback is essential if the practice is to serve its purpose. Which may be the long way around the barn to tell you that this short chapter offers some guided practice in recognizing useful characteristics of objectives and a wee bit of practice in editing a few that are in need of repair.

"Wait a minnit," I hear you saying. "How come the objective of the book wants me to be able to *recognize* useful characteristics and now you want me to do a *repair* job?" Good question. Answer: this is a practice chapter intended to help you sharpen up your discrimination skill. Asking you to repair a few objectives will cause you to pay closer attention to what you are learning to discriminate.

So sharpen your pencil and have at it.

Practice Items

Read the statements below. Place a check mark in the appropriate column to the right if a statement includes a performance, the conditions under which the performance is to appear, and/or a criterion by which successful performance of the objective can be assessed.

HINT: Always begin analyzing an objective by circling the performance. If no performance is stated, you need go no further.

	PERFORMANCE	CONDITIONS	CRITERION

1. Given a list of descriptions of human behavior, be able to differentiate (*sort*) between those that are normal and those that are psychotic.

2. Without regard to subject matter or grade level, be able to describe ten examples of school practices that promote learning and ten examples of school practices that retard or interfere with learning.

3. Given three hearings of a two-part polyphonic passage, be able to state whether a given melody, heard separately, was or was not one of the two heard polyphonically.

4. Given twenty minutes of instruction and a lab exercise, be able to develop an understanding of the difference between igneous, metamorphic, and sedimentary rocks. Criterion: 80 percent correct.

5. Be able to locate correctly the following four structures: ovary, ligaments of the ovary, fallopian tube, uterus.

Turn to page 108.

	PERFORMANCE	CONDITIONS	CRITERION

1. Given a list of descriptions of human behavior, be able to differentiate (*sort*) between
   those that are normal and those that are
   psychotic.   ✓   ✓   ___

2. Without regard to subject matter or grade
   level, be able to describe ten examples of
   school practices that promote learning and
   ten examples of school practices that retard
   or interfere with learning.   ✓   ✓   ✓

3. Given three hearings of a two-part polyphonic passage, be able to state whether a
   given melody, heard separately, was or was
   not one of the two heard polyphonically.   ✓   ✓   ___

Comment

1. This one describes a performance (sorting descriptions of behavior), and describes at least one condition (given a written list of descriptions of human behavior). It does not tell us how to know when the discrimination skill is good enough to be acceptable. What's that? You think a criterion is *implied*? Possibly. But think of the meaning of the word *implied*. An implication is a *suggestion* that is not openly or directly expressed. And if an implication is a suggestion rather than a specification, then you and I might differ in our understanding of that suggestion, depending on the knowledge, experience, and bias we bring to the act of implying. So perhaps a criterion is implied to you—and not to someone else. Since no criterion is *stated*, it doesn't matter whether I agree with the implication you read or not. Implication is not the same as explication, and in this case no criterion has been explicitly described.

2. Performance: describing. Conditions: any subject and any grade level. Criterion: descriptions of ten examples in each of the two categories.

3. This one also states performance and conditions. And, again, a criterion is *implied* but not stated. If there is not much chance that users would disagree on the nature of the implication, then the objective might be allowed to stand as is. But the possibility of misinterpretation could be reduced by adding a few words that clearly state the writer's intention regarding the criterion of acceptable performance.

	PERFORMANCE	CONDITIONS	CRITERION

4. Given twenty minutes of instruction and a lab exercise, be able to develop an understanding of the difference between igneous, metamorphic, and sedimentary rocks. Criterion: 80 percent correct.   ___ ___ ___

5. Be able to (locate) correctly the following four structures: ovary, ligaments of the ovary, fallopian tube, uterus.   ✓ ___ ✓

4. You didn't get caught on this false given, did you? It describes instructional procedure; it does *not* describe the conditions under which the performance is to occur. No performance is stated. And if it isn't, what possible meaning could there be to saying "80 percent correct"? It's rather like saying "Be able to understand the problems of the world. Criterion: 80 percent correct." Just labeling something a criterion doesn't make it one. On the other hand, I suppose you could argue that it is a criterion, but not a meaningful one in the present context.

5. This one states the main intent (but needs an indicator behavior to tell you how you will know the locating is correct) and tells you how well the performer must perform (four structures correctly located). But the lack of conditions might cause confusion. Is the objective talking about locating structures in medical photographs, in a deceased cat, or in a live woman? It would make a difference.

Turn to page 113.

Practice Items

Try a few more. If a statement includes a performance, conditions, or a criterion, place a check mark in the appropriate column to its right.

	PERFORMANCE	CONDITIONS	CRITERION
1. The student will learn the basic sanitary standards in the food industry, according to local and state codes.	___	___	___
2. Given the prices of two different-size packages of a product and the quantity of the product contained in each, be able to calculate the unit price of each and state which is the most economical purchase. Assume equal quality of products.	___	___	___
3. Given a table of figures indicating quantities that consumers will purchase at different prices, be able to draw a demand curve.	___	___	___
4. Write all of the privileges described in the Bill of Rights.	___	___	___
5. Be able to recognize correct and incorrect ways of placing and removing urinals for patients (a) who are helpless and (b) who can assist. SAMPLE TEST ITEM Look at the photographs in Envelope A and place an X on those showing incorrect ways of placing and removing urinals.	___	___	___

Turn to page 114.

PERFORMANCE CONDITIONS CRITERION

1. The student will learn the basic sanitary
   standards in the food industry, according to
   local and state codes.   ___ ___ ___

2. Given the prices of two different-size pack-
   ages of a product and the quantity of the
   product contained in each, be able to (calculate) the unit price of each and state which is
   the most economical purchase. Assume equal
   quality of products.   ✓   ✓   ___

3. Given a table of figures indicating quantities
   that consumers will purchase at different
   prices, be able to (draw) a demand curve.   ✓   ✓   ___

Comment

1. This is another of those nothing statements. So the student will learn. How nice. But what about the result of that learning? You haven't been let in on the secret. No performance, no need to look further.

2. Main intent: be able to calculate unit price. Conditions: given prices and quantities of two products. But how *well* must the calculating be done? You are not told. True, when dealing with arithmetic you may generally assume that all calculations must be correct, so you could say that a criterion is implied. But must I be correct every time? Wouldn't eight correct calculations out of ten be good enough (for the purpose being fulfilled by the objective)? How about six out of ten? What's your best offer? After all, always correct performance demands more skill than sometimes correct performance, and it might help to know which is desired. But, remember the rule: If there is room for disagreement, don't argue about it, fix it.

3. Same problem. Main intent and conditions are stated, but no explicit information is given about the desired quality of performance.

4. (Write) all of the privileges described in the Bill of Rights.   ✓ — ✓

5. Be able to (recognize) correct and incorrect ways of placing and removing urinals for patients (a) who are helpless and (b) who can assist.

SAMPLE TEST ITEM

Look at the photographs in Envelope A and place an X on those showing incorrect ways of placing and removing urinals.

4. This one looks clean and straightforward, but it could be improved. Main intent: recall privileges granted by the Bill of Rights. Indicator behavior: write. Criterion: *all* privileges must be written. If any are omitted, the performance is not good enough. But what about conditions? Do students have to perform without the use of references, or can they use notes? Can they have a copy of the Bill of Rights before them? The addition of a few words would help clarify the intent.

5. This one is pretty good. Main intent: discriminating (recognizing). Indicator behavior: marking photographs. Conditions: given photographs of subject situations. Criterion: not included—implied, perhaps, but not stated. How fine must the discriminating be for a student to be considered competent? You don't know.

Now try your hand at fixing objectives in need of some repair.

Turn to page 119.

Drafting Objectives Checklist

To help your objectives communicate, make sure that they answer the following questions in the affirmative:

1. *Is your main intent stated?*
2. *If the main intent is covert, is an indicator behavior stated?*
3. *Is that indicator behavior the simplest and most direct one you can think of?*
4. *Have you described what the learner will have, or be deprived of, when demonstrating achievement of the objective?*
5. *Have you described how well the learner must perform to be considered acceptable?*

An instructional objective:

Is a statement describing an intended outcome.

Describes intended outcome in terms of student performance.

Describes intended student performance at the time your influence over them ends (at the end of your instruction).

Describes student performance rather than teacher performance or instructional procedure.

EDITING PRACTICE

Below are some objectives in need of repair. They may contain unnecessary words, false givens, or meaningless phrases. Strike those out. They may lack one or more of the useful characteristics of an objective. Put those in. If you are not familiar with the subject of an objective and you need a condition or a criterion, make something up.

The checklist on the facing page may help you.

1. After three weeks of instruction on transportation, be able to classify transportation devices into those designed to move mainly (a) goods and (b) people.

2. Be able to change a tire on a car.

3. Be able to manifest a comprehensive understanding of the procedure for conducting an interview according to company standard CS-30.

4. Know how a toaster works.

5. Given a fifty-minute lecture, be able to take a patient's temperature.

When you have finished with your repairs, turn to page 120.

How'd You Do?

Your objectives will look somewhat different from mine. No matter. After all, there are lots of ways of saying the same thing. What matters is whether your objective is clear and contains the elements of a useful objective.

1. *After three weeks of instruction on transportation, be able to classify transportation devices into those designed to move mainly (a) goods and (b) people.*

This social-studies objective isn't too bad, but it begins with a false given. The words before the comma say nothing about what the student is expected to be able to do; the statement only informs you that there will be three weeks of instruction. But suppose it only *takes* five minutes of instruction? Or no instruction at all? When you allow instructional procedure to remain in an objective, you restrict the ingenuity and the creativity of the instructor in achieving the objective. So strike it out.

Now you can consider the essence. A performance is stated (classify). Since that is a covert main intent, it would help to add an indicator behavior. Another question: What will the learner have to work with when performing? A list of transportation devices? Photos of same? Nothing at all? It would help to say. Finally, how well must the student be able to classify? Add some sort of criterion. Yours might look like this:

Be able to classify a given list of common transportation devices into those designed to move mainly (a) goods and (b) people. Criterion: All items designed to move people must be classified correctly.

2. *Be able to change a tire on a car.*

Not bad. You know the performance, the performance is overt (visible), and you know a little about the conditions. But does this mean the students are to be able to change *any* tire on *any* car? Will they have to do this with bare hands and a tire iron? Can they take all day about it? As long as your version answers these questions, it would be acceptable. Here is how I would do it:

> *Given the tool kit issued with any model automobile less than ten years old and given a scissors jack and properly inflated spare tire, be able to replace the tire on any designated wheel within thirty minutes.*

3. *Be able to manifest a comprehensive understanding of the procedure for conducting an interview according to company standard CS-30.*

This one starts with some common gobbledegook that needs to be deleted. Rule: If you don't understand it, throw it out. In this case you have to decide what to mean by "understanding." You might have decided it means to be able to describe the procedure or to observe the procedure and recognize when it is being properly or improperly carried out. Or, you might have decided it means an ability to carry out the interview procedure. Since you are not told the meaning, you have to decide for yourself. (In real life you would perform a goal analysis or a similar procedure to derive the meaning appropriate to the situation.) My version would look something like this:

> *Be able to interview any prospective job applicant according to company standard CS-30. Criterion: four of five applicants interviewed according to the standard with no errors.*

4. Know how a toaster works.

You have the same problem here as in the previous practice item. What is "know" supposed to mean? To describe the workings? To be able to make one? To be able to fix one? Since you are not told, you have to decide for yourself. *I* decided that the meaningful skill here is being able to repair one, so I modified it this way:

> *Given all necessary tools, spare parts, and reference materials, be able to repair any brand of toaster. The repaired device must function according to manufacturer's specifications.*

5. Given a fifty-minute lecture, be able to take a patient's temperature.

Here again you have a false given. If you already knew how to do this, you would require no lecture, or no instruction at all. Since the purpose of an objective is to describe what you want students to be able to do, strike out the junk before the comma. That leaves you with "be able to take a patient's temperature." Not bad. Can you say anything more that would clarify the intent? You could indicate where the temperature would be taken, with what, and on what. On a real person? On a dummy? I would word it something like this:

> *Given any brand of oral thermometer, be able to take the oral temperature of any patient to within 0.5 degree accuracy. (Accuracy will be determined by comparing your readings with those of two instructors.)*

9 || Self-Test

On the following pages you will find a short self-test with which to try your skill at discriminating (identifying) the characteristics of objectives as discussed in this book. Answer all the questions, and then check your responses on pages 126–131.

For example, you might be given a statement such as the objective of this book, which, as you will recall, went like this:

Given any objective in a subject area with which you are familiar, in all instances be able to identify (label) *correctly the performance, the conditions, and the criterion of acceptable performance when any or all of those characteristics are present.*

You would be asked to indicate whether this objective had each of the three desired characteristics.

Incidentally, though I would like your skill to be perfect, I will have to adjust my criterion and settle for something less. Why? Because a condition of the objective calls for the skill to be performed on objectives "in a subject area with which you are familiar," and some of the items that follow may talk about subjects that are *un*familiar to you. So, to consider yourself competent you will have to decide correctly about at least forty-three of the fifty possible discriminations (i.e., forty-three of the fifty spaces correctly checked or left empty) while making no more than one error in the column labeled "Performance."

Have at it.

SELF-TEST

A. Do the following statements include performances? Does each at least tell what the learner will be doing when demonstrating achievement of the objective?

	States a performance	
	YES	NO

1. Understand the principles of salesmanship.   ___ ___

2. Be able to write three examples of the logical fallacy of the undistributed middle.   ___ ___

3. Be able to understand the meaning of Ohm's Law.   ___ ___

4. Be able to name the bones of the body.   ___ ___

5. Know the needs for nursing care associated with the stresses of life situations and with common aspects of illness.   ___ ___

6. Be able to really understand the plays of Shakespeare.   ___ ___

7. Be able to identify (*circle*) objectives that include a statement of desired performance.   ___ ___

8. Be able to recognize that the practical application of democratic ideals requires time, adjustment, and continuous effort.   ___ ___

9. Appreciate the ability of others, and perform as an intelligent spectator.   ___ ___

10. Be able to describe the indications for the use of a pacemaker.   ___ ___

B. Read the statements below. Place a check mark in the appropriate column to indicate any characteristic of a useful objective you find in each.

	PERFORMANCE	CONDITIONS	CRITERION
11. Demonstrate a knowledge of the principles of magnetism.	___	___	___
12. Be able to write an essay on evolution.	___	___	___
13. Using any reference materials, be able to name correctly every item shown on each of twenty blueprints.	___	___	___
14. Be able to write a description of the steps involved in making a blueprint.	___	___	___
15. On the 25-yard range, be able to draw your service revolver and fire five rounds from the hip within three seconds. At 25 yards all rounds must hit the standard silhouette target.	___	___	___
16. Be able to know <u>well</u> the cardinal rules of grammar.	___	___	___
17. Given an oral description of the events involved in an accident, be able to fill out a standard accident report.	___	___	___
18. Be able to write a coherent essay on the subject "How to Write Objectives for a Course in Law Appreciation." Course notes may be used, as well as any references.	___	___	___
19. Be able to develop logical approaches in the solution of personnel problems.	___	___	___
20. Without reference materials, be able to describe three common points of view regarding racial inferiority or superiority that are not supported by available research.	___	___	___

How'd You Do?

	States a performance	
	YES	NO

1. Understand the principles of salesmanship.   ✓ (NO)

2. Be able to (write) three examples of the logical fallacy of the undistributed middle.   ✓ (YES)

3. Be able to understand the meaning of Ohm's Law.   ✓ (NO)

4. Be able to (name) the bones of the body.   ✓ (YES)

5. Know the needs for nursing care associated with the stresses of life situations and with common aspects of illness.   ✓ (NO)

6. Be able to really understand the plays of Shakespeare.   ✓ (NO)

7. Be able to identify (*circle*) objectives that include a statement of desired performance.   ✓ (YES)

8. Be able to recognize that the practical application of democratic ideals requires time, adjustment, and continuous effort.   ✓ (NO)

9. Appreciate the ability of others, and perform as an intelligent spectator.   ✓ (NO)

10. Be able to (describe) the indications for the use of a pacemaker.   ✓ (YES)

A. Comment

1. A goal analysis would be in order here to determine the meaning of "understand."

2. You can tell whether someone is writing, so it qualifies as a performance.

3. Same problem as with Item 1.

4. Naming is a performance; you can tell when it is being done.

5. Same problem as with Item 1. An important goal, perhaps, but it does not qualify as an objective.

6. Underlining things doesn't make them any more specific— and that's <u>really true</u>.

7. Identifying is a covert performance that can be directly assessed by the single indicator behavior of circling or underlining or checking.

8. Again, perhaps an important thought, but what am I doing when recognizing that application of ideals requires time?

9. You didn't get caught on the "perform as an intelligent spectator" part of this, did you? What am I doing when performing? Shouting? Throwing bottles at an umpire? Sitting quietly? We are given nary a clue.

10. Describing is a performance. We are not told whether the describing must be oral or in writing, but either way the describing is a performance.

Performances are circled.
Conditions are underlined.
Criteria are in italics.

PERFORMANCE   CONDITIONS   CRITERION

11. Demonstrate a knowledge of the principles of magnetism.

    —   —   —

12. Be able to (write) an essay on evolution.

    ✓   —   —

13. Using any reference materials, be able to (name) *correctly every item shown on each of twenty blueprints.*

    ✓   ✓   ✓

14. Be able to (write) a description of the steps involved in making a blueprint.

    ✓   —   —

15. On the 25-yard range, be able to (draw) your service revolver (and fire five rounds from the hip) *within three seconds. At 25 yards all rounds must hit the standard silhouette target.*

    ✓   ✓   ✓

16. Be able to know *well* the cardinal rules of grammar.

    —   —   —

17. Given an oral description of the events involved in an accident, be able to (fill out) a standard accident report.

    ✓   ✓   —

B. Comment

11. *Demonstrate* is that trap word that often leads us to believe it is saying something specific.

12. Though you may read an implication that the writing must be done without reference materials, that condition is not stated. Neither are we told how the essay will be judged competent.

13. This one says something about performance, conditions, and criterion. It may be an objective that would appear at the bottom of an objectives hierarchy—that is, it may be a very low level skill—but it is an objective.

14. Here you may feel that a criterion is implied. It says to write the steps, and that could be read to mean "write all the steps correctly." And then, again, it might mean something else. If a few words will make the criterion clear, it is better to add them than to rely on inferences.

15. You may not agree with the purpose of the statement, but it is a good objective.

16. Italicizing *doesn't* make it so . . . or specific.

17. Again, you may read an implication of "without error." I wouldn't because I never assume that perfection is demanded unless it is explicitly specified. Perfection is seldom a realistic expectation.

PERFORMANCE CONDITIONS CRITERION

18. Be able to (write) a coherent essay on the sub-
    ject "How to Write Objectives for a Course
    in Law Appreciation." Course notes may be
    used as well as any references.   ✓   ✓   ___

19. Be able to develop logical approaches in the
    solution of personnel problems.   ___ ___ ___

20. Without reference materials, be able to (de-
    scribe) *three common points* of view regard-
    ing racial inferiority or superiority that are
    not supported by available research.   ✓   ✓   ✓

18. What does coherent mean? How would we recognize coherence if we saw it? We are not told.

19. Ah, well. Another nice-sounding statement, but not an objective.

20. This one is tricky. How well must the describing be done? Well, it has to describe three points of view not supported by research. Not much of a criterion, I'll admit, but a start.

HOW'D YOU DO?

To compare your responses against the criterion, do the following:

1. Circle any space that you left empty but that should have a check mark.
2. Circle the spaces you checked that you should have left empty.
3. Total the circled spaces (errors). If there are seven or fewer, AND if they include no more than one error in recognizing the presence or absence of a performance, consider yourself competent to recognize the presence or absence of the characteristics of a useful objective.

If you have more errors than specified in the criterion, you may want to review the chapter(s) dealing with the characteristic(s) on which we disagree.

One final thought. You are now ready to begin drafting your own objectives. May you be as picky with *them* as you have been with mine.

The Stoner
and the Stonees

"Professor, professor," cried the second-assistant digger-upper. "I think I've found something."

"Oh," replied the professor, raising his archeological head from the archeological dirt. "What is it?"

"It's a large stone with writing on it," enthused the excited assistant. "Maybe it's another part of the Great Recipe of Life."

"Let me see," said the professor as he raised his magnificent magnifying glass. "No, no, I think you're mistaken. See these markings? These are the names of people."

"People?" queried the assistant. "What people?"

"Hmm," replied the great one, profoundly. "It looks as though these are the names of people who contributed to the shaping and the fixing of a book."

"Why would anyone put their names in stone?" asked the assistant.

"Well," replied the professor, "it says here that the author didn't want anyone to forget just who it was that beat and bashed his words into presentable shape. He wanted the world to remember each and every one for what they did to his work."

"What *did* they do to it?" asked the assistant, edging closer for a better look.

"A number of things, according to these hieroglyphics. For example, it says here that Dave Cram, Margo Hicks, and John Warriner had something to do with making sure the manuscript hung together. *Continuity check* is the term he uses.

"Then he lists some people who helped test to make sure the book accomplished what it was supposed to. He calls that his *outcome check*. The names are Maryjane Rees, John

Alston, Joe De Hazes, Jeannette Hanne, Grant Bodwell, Michael Hanau, Jerry Tuller, and Jean White.

"After that he lists those who participated in a . . . an *attitude check,* apparently to make sure the book didn't contain any accidental turnoffs. Their names are Billy Koscheski, Elizabeth Epperson, Pauline Stone, Ann Redl, Dick Niedrich, Andy Stevens, Jane Kilkenny, and Marilyn McElhaney.

"Diane Pope is mentioned in deeply chiseled letters because she contributed a special example. Jeanne Mager is named as chief chiseler."

"Look at this!" cried the assistant. "Here are some words with a box chiseled around them. What do they say?"

"These," continued the professor as he tried to push his nose through his magnifying glass, "are the names of those who helped to test the cover design of the book. They are Frank Sedei, John Gray, Karen Schwartz, Sue Markle, Jim Straubel, Mike Nisos, Roger Kaufman, Margo Hicks, Bob Morgan, Al Collins, Joan Fleetwood, Stephen Daeschner, Bob Reichart, Harold Stolovitch, Wally Stauffer, and Jan Kaufman."

"And," continued the professor pomporiously, "here is a clump of names of those who tested the *new* cover designs. Looks like Clair Miller, Bill Valen, Dan Piskorik, Letitia Wiley, Carol Valen, Eileen Mager, Johan Adriaanse, Bob White, Jim Reed, Ethel Robinson, Fahad Omair, Phil Postel, Gerard Conesa, David Heath, and Paul Guersch."

"Gee whiz," exhaled the assistant. "That author didn't seem to know how to do *anything* by himself."

"Perhaps not," was the reply. "But it says here—you see these large chiselings—it says that *those who would do unto others should care what those others prefer.* That's why these people were asked to try on the manuscript. They helped to make it communicate better . . . and that's why they were stoned."